FUNdraising

For Nicholas,
who injects fun into everything he does

FUNdraising

50 Proven Strategies
for Successful School
Fundraisers

Frank Sennett

CORWIN PRESS
A SAGE Company
Thousand Oaks, CA 91320

For information:

Corwin Press
A Sage Publications Company
2455 Teller Road
Thousand Oaks,
   California 91320
www.corwinpress.com

Sage Publications India Pvt. Ltd.
B 1/I 1 Mohan Cooperative
   Industrial Area
Mathura Road, New Delhi 110 044
India

Sage Publications Ltd.
1 Oliver's Yard
55 City Road
London EC1Y 1SP
United Kingdom

Sage Publications Asia-Pacific Pte. Ltd.
33 Pekin Street #02–01
Far East Square
Singapore 048763

Printed in the United States of America.

Library of Congress Cataloging-in-Publication Data

Sennett, Frank.
FUNdraising : 50 proven strategies for successful school fundraisers/by Frank Sennett.
    p. cm.
Includes bibliographical references.
ISBN 978-1-4129-4981-1 (cloth)
ISBN 978-1-4129-4982-8 (pbk.)
    1. Educational fund raising. I. Title. II. Title: Fifty proven strategies for successful school fundraisers.

LC243.A1S46 2008
379.13—dc22   2007020185

This book is printed on acid-free paper.

07   08   09   10   11   10   9   8   7   6   5   4   3   2   1

Acquisitions Editor:	Elizabeth Brenkus
Editorial Assistants:	Desirée Enayati, Ena Rosen
Production Editor:	Veronica Stapleton
Copy Editor:	Paula L. Fleming
Typesetter:	C&M Digitals (P) Ltd.
Proofreader:	Dorothy Hoffman
Cover Designer:	Scott Van Atta

Table of Contents

Author's Note   x

Preface   xi

Acknowledgments   xiii

About the Author   xv

Introduction: Put the Fun Back in School
    FUNdraising   xvi
        A Tale of Two Pledge Drives   xvi
        A FUNdraising Manifesto   xviii

Part I. Stage Setters: Cornerstones of
    Successful Fundraising Campaigns   1

1. Exploring Ethics: Consider These Issues
    Before Launching a FUNdraiser   2

2. Don't Try This at School: Avoid These
    Fundraising Mishaps   8

3. Clicking for Cash: Crawl the Web for
    Delighted Donors   15

4. The Publicity Payoff: How to Generate
    Positive Press for Your FUNdraiser   27

Part II. 50 FUNdraising Ideas: Rake in the Bucks
    With These Creative Concepts   31

5. Excellent Extravaganzas   32
        No. 1. "Educational Film Festival." Screen a
        series of unintentionally hilarious educational
        movies from bygone eras.   32

No. 2. "Inspiring Expositions." Put on an "inspiration expo" replete with local experts on fascinating subjects. 33

No. 3. "Auctioning Experiences." Build buzz for silent and live auctions by letting folks bid on amazing outings. 34

No. 4. "Double the Auction Fun." When a bidder wins the hottest auction item, wow the crowd by putting up an extra one for sale. 37

No. 5. "Housing Markets." Host home tours with a twist. 38

No. 6. "Pampering Moms." Give the women of the school community a well-deserved break for fun and games. 40

No. 7. "Digging for Diamonds." A sandbox full of jewelry makes for glitzy, gritty fun. 42

No. 8. "Tea Partying." Leaf through these rich and tasty themes. 43

No. 9. "Dance Fever." Relive high school memories with an adult prom. 44

No. 10. "The Pour House." Raise a glass for students at a wine tasting. 46

No. 11. "Daring to Sing." Tune in to a karaoke challenge. 49

No. 12. "Treasure Hunting." Send donors off on a wild scavenger hunt. 50

6. Starring Students **52**

No. 13. "Spellbinding Solicitations." Host a student spell-a-thon or "celebrity" spelling bee featuring administrators, teachers, and other prominent smarty-pants locals. 52

No. 14. "Paging Profits." Uncover nifty ways to jazz up your book fair. 54

No. 15. "Model Behavior." Put on a stylish school fashion show. 57

No. 16. "Record-Setting Haul." Enlist students to set a world record. 60

No. 17. "Freeform Fundraising." Maximize student participation with a "do-your-own-thing-a-thon." 62

7. Sporting Chances   **64**

No. 18. "Tee Time." Drive up receipts with a
variation on the classic golf tournament.   64

No. 19. "Drop the Balls." When numbered
golf balls fall from the sky, schools win.   66

No. 20. "Hoop Dreaming." Score with a
three-on-three basketball tournament.   68

No. 21. "Mascot Madness." Have a field day
with the district's costumed characters.   70

8. Artistic Attractions   **71**

No. 22. "Appraising Treasures." Throw an
Antiques Roadshow-style event at
which people can pay to have cherished
heirlooms appraised.   71

No. 23. "Picture This." Target discerning donors
with a student art show and sale.   72

No. 24. "Chair-itable Artworks." Auction off
furniture painted by students and other
local artists.   73

No. 25. "Feeling Scrappy." Make memories—and
money—with a school scrapbooking night.   75

No. 26. "Playing Around." Delight young and old
by auctioning off fancy playhouses.   76

No. 27. "Throwing a Disc." Record and sell instant
CDs of musical performances.   78

No. 28. "Band on the Run." Set up musical
performances where people will least
expect them.   79

9. Animal Antics   **81**

No. 29. "Flamingo Flocking." Plant plastic pink
flamingoes in the yards of unsuspecting
victims—for a price.   81

No. 30. "Living the Wild Life." Enchant the
community by displaying whimsical animal
sculptures all over town.   83

No. 31. "Circus Maximus." Invite the big top to
town to perform for your school.   85

No. 32. "Pet Smart." Host a dog- and cat-friendly
celebration.   89

No. 33. "Hitting the Spot." Play cow, horse, or chicken bingo to enjoy the smell of money.   90

10. Service Smiles   **93**

No. 34. "Recycling Revenues." Bag profits by providing specialty recycling services to the community.   93

No. 35. "Cleaning Up." Pitch in around town on yard work and chores for a fee.   95

No. 36. "Baby Booming." Brand your school as the go-to spot for child care during citywide events.   97

No. 37. "Classic Car Car Wash." Buff up the standard car wash by catering to sweet rides.   98

No. 38. "Send in the Dads." Enlist fathers and other men in the school community to team up for a memorable event.   99

No. 39. "Celebrity Service." Enlist prominent locals and district employees to serve meals at a restaurant's school night.   100

No. 40. "Giving Directions." Hire out teens and adults to flag shoppers into stores.   102

11. Seasonal Successes   **104**

No. 41. "Scare Up a Maze." Find money by losing visitors in a haunted Halloween maze.   104

No. 42. "Seasonal Singing." Get into the holiday spirit by booking groups of carolers all over town.   106

No. 43. "Gingerbread Housing." Tempt holiday revelers with a parade of deliciously decorated homes.   107

No. 44. "Polar Plunge." Heat up donations by dunking local notables in cold water.   108

12. Cash Collecting   **109**

No. 45. "A Home Run." Raffle off a dream house to make your fundraising dreams come true.   109

No. 46. "Naming Games." Sell naming rights to small school projects and reap big windfalls.   111

No. 47. "Give 'em the Boot." Enlist crossing guards
and other members of the school
community to ask passing motorists to drop
donations into an outstretched boot.   113
No. 48. "Fee Parking." Allow teens to personalize
school parking spaces for an annual surcharge.   114
No. 49. "Your Money or Your Time." Offer
community members multiple ways to give.   115
No. 50. "Stunts Doubling." Cap off a successful
fundraising effort by performing a silly stunt.   116

References   **118**

Author's Note

When it comes to fundraising, ethical considerations are critically important. That's why "Exploring Ethics" is the first chapter of the book. But legal issues sometimes must be addressed before moving forward with a given event as well. So whenever applicable, review laws governing games of chance, the serving of alcohol, and any other areas of potential legal concern.

Preface

M any fundraising guides exhaustively explore the basics of recruiting volunteers, setting up a handful of standard events, executing them with precision, and keeping close track of the cash they generate.

And there's absolutely nothing wrong with that.

But you're holding something quite different in your hands.

This is an idea book for leaders in the school community who can oversee a basic fundraiser in their sleep—yet long to wake up to creative new approaches and clever twists on classic events. (It's also for newcomers who want to make a quick, positive impact by exposing the school's veteran fundraisers to fun, fresh concepts.)

The 50 ideas are supported with lists of potential outside partners/sponsors, savvy organizing tips, and real-life examples of administrators, teachers, parents, students, and local supporters who have pulled off popular and lucrative fundraisers.

If you want to host events that raise spirits along with money; if you want the community to view your fundraisers as necessary entertainments and services instead of unnecessary evils; and if you want to look back at your school's revenue-raising efforts with pride rather than relief that they're over, well then . . .

This may be exactly the book you've been waiting for.

ADDED ATTRACTIONS

Several nonprofit educational organizations publish low- or no-cost guides that outline the basics of setting up a school fundraiser:

- ⑨ *PTA Fundraising Essentials* is available to local PTA chapters through www.pta.org. (The site also features articles on fundraising fundamentals.)

- ● National Association of Elementary School Principals members can access "A Principal's Guide to Fundraising" and related articles through www.naesp.org.
- ● The National Association of Secondary School Principals publishes *Fundraising: Not Just a Cakewalk Anymore,* which promises to take readers "step-by-step through every phase of organizing and carrying out a successful fundraiser." It's available through www.principals.org.
- ● Download the free, 103-page *New York City Charter Schools Fundraising Guidebook* at www.nycchartercenter.org/2006_Fundraising_Guidebook.pdf.

Acknowledgments

I'll start with a special thank you to Lizzie Brenkus both for asking me to write this book and for being one cool cat. Further thanks go to Robb, Hudson, Diane, Desirée, Veronica, the crack marketing team, and all of the other wonderful folks at Corwin Press who make these projects possible. They are a treat to work with. I'm also indebted to the innovative educators whose fundraising ideas inform the text; they're an inspiring bunch. (That's especially true of DonorsChoose.org creator Charles Best and John Deasy, who pioneered a school fundraising equity fund in Santa Monica, California.) And, as always, I'm grateful to my family for their continued love and support.

Corwin Press gratefully acknowledges the contributions of the following individuals:

Mary Ann Burke, Grants Coordinator
Oakland Unified School District
Oakland, California

Gerard A. Dery
Director, Zone 1, National Association of Elementary
    School Principals
Principal, Nessacus Regional Middle School
Dalton, Massachusetts

Gary Lee Frye, Director of Development and Grants
Lubbock-Cooper Independent School District
Lubbock, Texas

Joen Painter, Education Consultant
Yuma, Arizona

Bonnie Tryon
Director, School Administrators Association of New York
Principal, Golding Elementary School
Cobleskill, New York

Steve Zsiray, Principal and CEO
InTech Collegiate High School
North Logan, Utah

About the Author

Frank Sennett earned his fiction MFA from the University of Montana and now teaches in the UCLA Extension Writers' Program. He served as editor of the K–12 journal *Curriculum Review* for a decade. His other Corwin Press books are *101 Stunts for Principals to Inspire Student Achievement* and *400 Quotable Quotes From the World's Leading Educators.* To book Frank for a session on creative school fundraising or educational stunts, please contact the Corwin Press Speakers' Bureau. Call 1-800-818-7243 and press 5.

Introduction

Put the Fun Back in School FUNdraising

I love to write books, but I'll let you in on a secret: Radio remains my favorite medium. It possesses an enchanting ability to spark the imagination instantly—but only in close collaboration with the listener, who must provide the mental pictures to go with the words and music.

Here's all it takes to make great radio: open minds reaching out to each other across the ether. One of my broadcast heroes, Ken Nordine, opened his long-running public radio show, *Word Jazz*, with a phrase that sums up that interactive entertainment experience wonderfully well: "Stare with your ears."

There's a lot of mindless junk on the air these days, of course, but radio's possibilities remain nearly endless. Array a few creative people around a microphone, and they can conjure entire worlds that captivate thousands of listeners with little or no budget for special effects. Remember, Orson Welles's radio production of *War of the Worlds* created far more of a cultural stir than the blockbuster film version starring Tom Cruise.

A TALE OF TWO PLEDGE DRIVES

How does this tie into school fundraising? Well, most of my broadcast experience lies in public radio. As a result, I've volunteered for plenty of pledge drives over the years. And the two stations with which I'm most familiar couldn't be more different in their approaches to the task. The contrast provides a great lesson for school leaders setting out to raise money for their educational endeavors.

One station assumes that listeners hate pledge drives and operates accordingly. Officials promise to reduce the number of fundraising days if early membership renewals hit a certain level. Many of the prerecorded promotions are humorous and inventive—and the on-air folks make the case for contributing in a professional manner. But the pledge drives always have about them the air of dreary obligation. Announcers regularly apologize for soliciting donations and frame pledge drives as a necessary evil.

The other station takes the opposite approach. Staffers view pledge week as a fun way to connect with listeners and celebrate their connection to the community. Special guests regularly drop in for a chat—in fact, I once scored a pledge-drive interview with public radio's Dr. Science (he told listeners he would have beaten the late Mr. Wizard in a wrestling match). And the estimated 300 volunteers who take the phone pledges every year get in on the act with an array of silly-sounding noisemakers.

Instead of just offering tried-and-true (and tired) pledge premiums such as mugs and T-shirts, this station asks loyal supporters to donate oddball prizes, including live goats, handmade toys, residential moving services, and "anti-road-rage" lavender sachets. In addition to the 2,000 premiums it averages every year, the station caps off pledge week with Pet Wars, during which listeners call in with donations in honor of their dogs, cats, ferrets—you name it (Szpaller, 2005).

The latter station broadcasts from a smaller city than the former one. But in one week, it raises more money than the other station does in two. It isn't that one community is naturally inclined to support public radio less than the other, nor are the broadcasters at the pledge-happy station more passionate about their jobs.

It's just that the more financially successful station sees pledge week as an opportunity—to have fun, to connect, to take a break from the same old, same old—instead of as a chore. The amazing result: listeners in that community actually look forward to the event.

The lesson is simple: if you treat school fundraising as drudgery, the community will agree with you. But if you get excited about FUNdraising and maximize each event's potential for education, outreach, and plain old good times, the buzz likely will prove infectious—while participation levels and receipts soar to new heights.

We've seen a backlash in recent years against the old-fashioned product sales that force parents to twist arms at the office until colleagues buy items they don't want or need in hopes that others will return the favor when their children's fundraisers roll around. Of course, some school sales drives remain welcome traditions in their communities—and more power to those exceptional exceptions, I say.

But where that backlash exists, it isn't against schools or even fundraisers. Some communities, shell-shocked by a never-ending stream of sales, have adopted an annual cash-contribution model instead. This shows that participating school families are still willing to support education; they just don't want to be harassed in the process.

Wouldn't it be better, though, if schools entertained and delighted those communities with their fundraisers instead of trading annoying sales for obligatory pledges?

There's a lot of goodwill out there for schools, and they still have an important cultural-enrichment role to play in their communities. Please keep those heartening facts in mind as you peruse the following pages for fundraising ideas everyone can get excited about.

A FUNDRAISING MANIFESTO

Your event just might be a FUNdraiser if it does one or more of the following:

- Offers an experience so compelling people would show up even if it wasn't in support of a good cause.
- Enhances the cultural life of the overall community.
- Provides a service that's both needed and desired.
- Improves the school experience of student participants.
- Leaves attendees with a smile and a good memory.
- Puts a creative twist on a classic fundraising idea.
- Showcases the school community's distinctive talents.
- Clearly explains to donors where their money will go.
- Generates enthusiastic local media coverage.
- Becomes a popular (and lucrative) annual happening.

- ⑤ Helps school families spend more enjoyable time together instead of burdening them with dreaded sales chores.
- ⑤ Raises the school's positive profile among people not directly tied to the institution, thus expanding its base of support.
- ⑤ Taps into the increasing number of Web funding sources for pain-free program support.

Part I

Stage Setters

Cornerstones of Successful Fundraising Campaigns

CHAPTER ONE

Exploring Ethics

Consider These Issues Before
Launching a FUNdraiser

E thical issues arise in connection with school fundraisers all
the time. Should alcohol be served at shindigs supporting the
education of children? Should schools profit from donkey basketball, cow bingo, and other activities that employ animals? Where
does one draw the line on games of chance—at teddy bear raffles,
bingo games, casino nights, or beyond? Are corporate sponsorships
ever acceptable for campus events? How are student needs being
met by a given fundraiser?

Those are all important questions. But school leaders must
come up with their own answers to them based on applicable
laws, district policies, the tenor of the community, past fundraising experiences, and gut instinct.

It might prove useful for us to explore a particularly potent
pair of fundraising ethics issues here, however: the propriety of
candy sales, and the troubling fact that private donations tend to
increase the resource gap between rich and poor schools.

LOSING AT CANDY LAND

At a time of rising childhood obesity rates and mounting pressure
to improve school nutrition, many critics see the continuation of

school candy sales as both hypocritical and dangerous. Those critics have a point.

Let's consider the main arguments for allowing candy sales:

- ⑨ **They bring in a lot of money.** That's true, but booze and drugs would bring in even more. So this isn't an ethically sound defense.
- ⑨ **It's tradition!** Again, true, but many once-cherished traditions fall by the wayside as social mores change. For example, a story in Chapter 2, "Don't Try This at School," describes a student who got suspended for waving around a chocolate gun—an item the school had been selling at fundraisers for several decades. Not anymore.
- ⑨ **Kids love candy, and if we don't sell it to them, someone else will.** As someone who used to duck out of high school study halls to grab an apple fritter at a shop next door called the Sugar Shack, I'm in no position to question the veracity of that assertion. But schools are supposed to set a good example, and taking advantage of unhealthy cravings doesn't send the best message.

Sweet Nothings?

On the other hand, banishing sweets from campus strikes many folks as unrealistic—and such moves certainly invite backlash from both students and parents.

Sometimes even state legislators—and the media—get involved. Consider the case of the "Safe Cupcake" law passed by the Texas Legislature in 2005. Representative Jim Dunnam pushed the legislation through after hearing about a parent's being banned from bringing pizzas into a school classroom on his child's birthday, the *Los Angeles Times* reported (Mehta, 2006). Said Dunnam, "There's a lot of reasons our kids are getting fat. Cupcakes aren't one of them." In 2006, Massachusetts legislators battled over a proposal to bar elementary school cafeterias from serving Fluffernutter sandwiches, the *New York Times* reported (Zezima, 2006). The pro-Fluff forces prevailed, in part because the gooey marshmallow substance has been manufactured in the state since 1920.

Although a ban on candy sales may prove unpalatable, cutting back on the snack attacks shouldn't be impossible. One of my goals with this book was to spread the word on low-calorie fundraisers. I did include a few themed meal events but passed on writing up the lucrative pizza, hot dog, and doughnut "eat-a-thon" that took place at Dundee-Crown High School in Illinois a few years back (Gaunt, 2004).

So the next time a school group can't think of an alternative to peddling sugary treats, let them chew on the ideas in Part II, "50 FUNdraising Ideas: Rake in the Bucks With These Creative Concepts," until they find an event they like. School administrators and PTA/PTO boards also might consider limiting groups to one food-focused fundraiser a year. Here's another compromise idea: require all candy sales to feature healthy alternative snacks as well.

GOOD ETHICS = GOOD MARKETING

There might be one way to institute a ban on candy sales without taking a huge financial hit or suffering a big backlash: make the antiobesity angle part of your marketing pitch.

Whenever you throw a fundraiser in the year after the ban, tell potential donors something like this: "We've kicked the junk food habit. Please help keep us healthy by participating in this fun, calorie-free event." The beautiful part of this appeal is that it gives members of the school community another altruistic reason to contribute. They can enjoy the photo scavenger hunt or classic auto car wash, all the while thinking of their donation as a blow against obesity, too.

A state ban recently forced the Associated Student Body of West Valley High in Riverside, California, to give up selling snacks in its school store. The group concentrated on selling advertising banners to local businesses instead, the *Press-Enterprise* reported (Ayala, 2006), in part by explaining the school's healthy eating kick. The color ads hang from a school fence along a busy thoroughfare. Students planned to sell up to 70 of the banners for $500 or $750 to replace the $35,000 lost from junk-food sales.

This type of approach works even better when it comes directly from children who voluntarily give up their candy sales after learning how unhealthy they are. That's what happened recently in Fort Lauderdale at Florida's North Side Elementary.

Participation in a "Schools of Wellness" initiative meant the kids soaked up plenty of lessons on good nutrition. Those lessons sunk in so well that fourth and fifth graders raising cash for a trip to Washington, D.C., refused to sell snacks, the *Sun-Sentinel* reported (Shores, 2006). "If they tell us to not eat junk food and then after school we sell it, that disobeys what they said," one student reasoned. Added another smart cookie, "We want the other kids to be healthy."

The truth about unhealthy eating set those students free. As with so many problems, increased education may prove critical to solving this one in the long term.

ADDED ATTRACTION

⑤ The Center for Science in the Public Interest published *Sweet Deals: School Fundraising Can Be Healthy and Profitable* in early 2007. The free 70-page guide is available for download at http://cspinet.org/new/pdf/schoolfundraising.pdf.

EQUITABLE FUNDING SOLUTIONS

Funding inequities remain a scourge of the U.S. educational system. Unfortunately, fundraisers can broaden already wide resource disparities among schools. A growing number of affluent schools are addressing this ethical concern head-on, as we soon will see.

In the summer of 2005, the *New York Daily News* (Lucadamo, 2005) compared the relative success parent associations at two public schools had in generating educational dollars during the previous school year. P.S. 6 on Manhattan's wealthy Upper East Side brought in $448,000 from parents. Intermediate School 275 in impoverished Harlem netted $551. That translated into $250 per student at P.S. 6 and 62 cents per pupil at I.S. 275. Said one district official, "Life isn't fair. How do you begrudge parents for giving to their own school?"

No one begrudges parents for supporting their children's schools, of course. But some enlightened educational leaders have taken to heart the moral imperative to provide students in their districts with equal access to program funding. In 2004, for instance, California's Santa Monica-Malibu Unified School District created a shared fund, called the Equity Fund, that takes a 15 percent cut of all private donations to its schools and redistributes that money on the basis of need.

The fund was the brainchild of Superintendent John Deasy, a true educational visionary who went on to become CEO of Maryland's Prince George's County Public Schools. "There were enormous disparities in fundraising amongst various parts of the school community," Deasy recalled on National Public Radio's *Talk of the Nation* (Conan, 2006). "You would have one school that would raise $32 over the course of the year per pupil, and another school $1,003 per pupil."

To overcome sometimes-fierce resistance in wealthier neighborhoods, Deasy and his allies pitched the fund as a way for the 13,000-student, 16-school district to come together. "While there are many schools, it is one community," he said. "All of our youth actually graduate from one community and participate in our democracy. And the fundamental notion is that every student gets, in my opinion, the right to the same quality of educational experience, no matter their geography" (Conan, 2006).

There's also a compelling practical argument to be made for equal distribution of fundraising proceeds. "In reality, we're also going to be all working together in five years," Deasy told NPR's *All Things Considered* (Kahn, 2004). "I want the people who are taking care of me in the health care profession, flying my planes, fixing my cars, and taking care of my banking to have the exact same opportunities and skill sets."

Opponents called the proposal a "gift tax" and said it would discourage donations to well-off schools. But after the board approved the plan, fundraising actually increased throughout the community. In its first year, the Equity Fund brought in more than $170,000, the *Washington Post* reported (Anderson, 2006). The district has been able to significantly reduce funding disparities ever since.

Portland, Oregon's district has had a more limited fundraising equity fund in place since 1995. Under the Rose City's model, private donations that schools allocate to pay for instructional services get pooled. The money is then awarded by the Portland Schools Foundation in the form of educational challenge grants.

"We've seen great results" in terms of higher math and literacy achievement at targeted schools, the foundation's director told the *Los Angeles Times* (Groves, 2004).

Such equity funds only fix inequalities in a single district, of course, while schools in neighboring communities may face even greater disparities. But if more communities would explore this option, perhaps we could someday witness the creation of state-wide equity funds. In lieu of miraculous changes in government school-funding policies, it's something to hope for.

BUILDING FOUNDATIONS

In addition to redistributing a portion of school fundraising proceeds, Santa Monica-Malibu's Equity Fund became a destination for corporate donors as well. As you're likely aware, many communities have established district education foundations to solicit such contributions and hold independent fundraisers. That money often goes directly to local schools in the form of grants (as in Portland, Oregon), creating some funding equity.

California alone now boasts more than 550 education foundations. They raise and distribute more than $50 million a year. As one organization's president told the *Ventura County Star*, "The foundation is about raising all the boats in the harbor. It's not just my kid's school, or my kid's class, or my kid's sport. The foundation is the only one that can do districtwide programs" (Moore, 2005).

ADDED ATTRACTION

⑤ For details on setting up a public school foundation, check out fundraising consultant Stanley Levenson's *Big-Time Fundraising for Today's Schools* (Corwin Press, 2006), which also explores the educational grant-writing process.

C H A P T E R   T W O

Don't Try This at School

Avoid These Fundraising Mishaps

Chapter 4, "The Publicity Payoff," proffers pointers on securing positive press for your school's fundraisers. But as most educators know, avoiding bad publicity is also crucial to putting on a successful event. With that in mind, read on for some past fundraising mishaps—along with lessons worth taking away from them.

DISARMING DISASTERS

The Germantown, Wisconsin, district halted a high school band booster club's sale of fishing kits that included six-inch fillet knives, the *Milwaukee Journal Sentinel* reported (Maller, 2004a). A truck driver delivering the 2,200 kits pointed out the situation to the principal. "It seemed like a kit with a fishing lure, fish batter, a recipe book, and a videotape," said the band leader, who ended up storing the items in his garage. "We were not aware of the fillet knife. It was there, but it wasn't obvious. I didn't realize it until the truck came around." The embarrassing incident, which drew national attention, was capped off by the school board president's calling it "an act of extreme dumbness." On the bright side, this story sounds like perfect material for a Funky Winkerbean comic strip.

In a truly bizarre story, a student at Union High in Clarion County, Pennsylvania, faced a disorderly conduct charge after he waved around a chocolate gun on a school bus, the *Pittsburgh Post-Gazette* reported (Hernan, 2000). The teen was pointing the candy weapon at laughing classmates when the bus driver spotted the scene in his rearview mirror and stopped the vehicle in the middle of traffic to confiscate the banned item. Even though the chocolate gun was purchased during a fundraiser for the school's Spanish club, the teen still faced charges. The district banned future sales of the candy guns, which had been offered for decades at fundraisers.

Lessons

Know exactly what student, parent-teacher, and booster groups plan to sell. If an item violates school policy, help find an acceptable alternative. By the way, the fishing-kit controversy cited above was resolved when the district allowed the fundraiser to proceed as long as parents—not students—distributed the fishing kits to buyers (Maller, 2004b). The incident also led the principal to require all future fundraisers to secure administrative approval before going forward. That's a rule well worth considering.

JOKES THAT DRAW JEERS

You know those calendars for which members of community groups pose nude (or nearly so) behind strategically placed props in the name of good-humored fundraising? Well, according to the report in Carroll, Iowa's *Daily Times Herald,* Roger Schmiedeskamp didn't even doff all his duds for his Rotary Club's calendar, and he got into a bunch of hot water anyway (Burns, 2006a). The Manning, Iowa, schools superintendent wore a swimsuit for his photo. The shot of him, taken at a studio, was digitally inserted into a picture of an old school desk. Several parents soon raised a ruckus. "In my mind, that is soft-core porn," said one incensed dad. "They're giving the impression that he's naked behind a desk." But the board backed its superintendent. Added Schmiedeskamp, "I wouldn't do it again because of the backlash in the community, but I still do not think it was wrong."

Elsewhere, some 25 students mounted a protest at Arcadia High in Phoenix after administrators canceled a "servant/slave" auction scheduled as a senior class fundraiser. "The sale of any human beings, under any circumstances, is just plain wrong," one teacher told the *Arizona Republic* (Ryman, 2003). Sounds like a reasonable response. But the teens were desperate to bring back a tradition that had seen students from previous classes forced to wear dog collars and leashes to school.

Lessons

Before engaging in a humorous fundraising ploy, be sure the school community will cheer instead of jeer. Regularly review long-standing fundraisers as well; events deemed acceptable in your community years ago may not pass muster today. Ironically, the worldwide publicity generated by the calendar story cited above helped the local Rotary Club sell out its 2007 edition; unfortunately, the school district received no direct contributions from the racy sale (Burns, 2006b).

WITH FRIENDS LIKE THESE . . .

The Las Vegas tourism slogan is "What happens in Vegas stays in Vegas." But a Sin City strip club's fundraiser for local schools drew unwanted national attention to the Clark County School District, the Associated Press reported (Nakashima, 2006). Scores Las Vegas raised $2,500 from an event at which dancers dressed (and then undressed) as schoolgirls, teachers, and librarians. One flier promised "detention for everyone who has been bad!" The club passed the cash on to the county's Public Education Foundation, which happily accepted it. But at least one district official wasn't pleased that the independent nonprofit group took the money, telling a reporter, "The donation was made to the foundation, and for the inner workings of how that functions, you can contact the foundation again." She also pointedly noted that the district had not known about the event and found the advertisement offensive. Translation: Please don't smear the school system's good name for something over which it had no control.

It might seem like piling on, but here's one more Las Vegas story worth sharing. Back in 2000, dozens of community members protested the school board's decision to name a new school Wendell P. Williams Elementary after a state legislator with a checkered past, which included a bankruptcy filing and falling $52,000 behind in child-support payments, the *Las Vegas Review-Journal* reported (Bach, 2003). The school was named after Williams anyway. In 2003, when the lawmaker found himself the subject of two investigations—one looking at his participation in a possibly irregular hiring process, and another examining time cards indicating he may have been paid for city work while he was attending state legislative sessions—the naming issue flared right back up. Said one community activist who'd vocally opposed the board's decision in 2000, "I told you so."

Lessons

If your district receives funding from independent school foundations, meet with them to set ground rules about acceptable, and unacceptable, events and donors. If you sell naming rights to schools, athletic fields, or any other facilities, run background checks on the people who want to be immortalized—and don't sign on the dotted line if too many red flags pop up. Also, include clauses in all naming-rights contracts that enable the district to rename the facilities without returning the money if the original donors are later convicted of crimes. (Explore this issue with legal counsel before proceeding.)

GOING OFF HALF-BAKED

Teens and bake sales don't always mix. Take, for instance, the junior at Ohio's Westerville North High who allegedly cooked up marijuana-laced Rice Krispies treats for a class trip fundraiser ("Student Facing," 2002). Or the teen in Lueneburg, Germany, who sent several teachers to the hospital by serving them a fundraiser cake infused with hashish ("Teen Admits," 2004). And let's not forget the enterprising senior at Weston, Florida's Cypress Bay High who was nabbed while allegedly conducting his own pot-brownie bake sale outside the cafeteria—and making a killing at $5 a square, the *Sun-Sentinel* reported (Ryan & Kaye, 2005).

Lessons

It's probably best to have parents prepare—and personally deliver—any bake sale treats. Sending home fliers on safe food-handling techniques might not be a bad idea, either. And if you do want to get students in on the act, ask them to bake their treats in the school cafeteria under adult supervision.

CELEBRATING THE WRONG CELEBRITY

When Ogden, Utah's DaVinci Academy advertised that comedian Jon Stewart would appear at its annual fundraising dinner gala, the charter school expected about 900 people to show up at $50 a head. They probably would have hit that attendance figure, if DaVinci hadn't accidentally booked Chicago motivational speaker and pro wrestler Jon A. Stewart instead of the star of Comedy Central's *The Daily Show With Jon Stewart*. The school went ahead with an event featuring local performers but provided refunds to ticket buyers who couldn't do without Stewart, the *Deseret Morning News* reported (Erickson, 2006).

"I thought it was a little elaborate for me," Jon A. Stewart told the *Chicago Sun-Times* (Hussain, 2006) after it became clear there was a mix-up with the school. "I actually started to feel bad for them." It's hard not to chuckle just a bit about the incident, though.

Lessons

Make sure you're getting the special guests you expect, and double-check references of speaker's bureaus before signing con-tracts. Also, beware of talent agents who supposedly represent popular bands from the 1950s and 1960s but actually only license the names and send out acts with no original members. Other potential pitfalls: motivational speakers who delve into material too intense for young audiences (such as the raw tales of a recovered addict) and those looking to sneak in inappropriate religious-themed messages.

MAKING A BAD BET

Stoneleigh Elementary in Towson, Maryland, long enjoyed fundraising success with its PTA teddy bear raffle, which brought in as much as $800 a year. But the fun and lucrative tradition came to an abrupt end in 2005 when the new principal pointed out that Baltimore County bans all games of chance from its school properties. "My head understands, but my heart is very disappointed," an organizer told the *Baltimore Sun* (Kay, 2005). But raffles are not allowed in district schools, even with such cuddly prizes.

Lessons

Review state and local laws on charitable games of chance—as well as district and school policies—before hosting even the most innocuous gambling-themed fundraiser. But if the school community approves of a proposed event that isn't allowed on school property, consider putting it on at another location. And if district rules on the issue seem outmoded, you can always lobby for a change or exemption. As one former Baltimore County superintendent said regarding the raffle cited above, "It's hard to pick on teddy bears" (Kay, 2005).

SUFFERING FROM STICKY FINGERS

Stories of school secretaries, PTA/PTO treasurers, principals, and teachers pilfering fundraiser proceeds for their own use aren't common—but they're not nearly as rare as they should be, either. The Parent Teacher Organization of Cypress School in Tulare, California, found that out the hard way when a treasurer pocketed more than $4,000 in donations by depositing presigned checks from the organization into a personal bank account. "It's not an excuse, but we're all volunteers, and we're busy," the Cypress principal told the *Tulare Advance-Register* (Thompson, 2004). "Things get relaxed a little bit."

Lessons

That story stood out because the school and the PTO learned so much from the thefts—and they put all of the lessons into action. After admitting that a relaxed state of affairs opened the door to embezzlement, the principal added, "They're not relaxed anymore" (Thompson, 2004). Schools and other fundraising groups should consider emulating the steps Cypress took to tighten their financial controls. These included requiring two signatures on checks drawn on the organization's account, regular formal audits, informally allowing any curious member to examine the books, removing some of the temptation by never leaving fundraising cash unsecured after fundraisers, making sure at least two people are in charge of taking money during events, and putting the guidelines in writing. School districts have a duty to ensure accountability and compliance in the management of all fiscal resources, including those brought in by fundraisers. Issuing guidelines modeled after the tips above would be a step in the right direction.

SCRAPPING THE SCRIP

California-based Scrip Advantage, Inc., used to sell millions of dollars of discounted retailer gift certificates to schools and other nonprofits. Those groups then sold the certificates at face value during fundraisers. The system worked until Scrip Advantage stopped shipping out scrip the groups had paid for. As of late 2006, the company had ceased operations and left schools and other organizations with nearly $7 million in unfulfilled orders, the *Fresno Bee* reported (Clough, 2006). Other scrip programs remain popular, but this sad story underscores the need to check the financial stability of any provider before sending in money.

LIVING WITH MURPHY'S LAW

If these unfortunate anecdotes help head off a fundraising hassle or two, they've served their purpose. But remember, no matter how well prepared you think you are, mistakes are bound to happen once in a while. When they do, keep your chin up; event snafus aren't the end of the world.

CHAPTER THREE

Clicking for Cash

Crawl the Web for Delighted Donors

C ouple your creative live events with innovative online campaigns for a powerful one-two fundraising punch. Here are
some ideas and resources to get you started, followed by interviews
with the founders of DonorsChoose and Classroom Wishlist, two
useful sites that link individual educators and schools to funding
for projects small and large.

As fundraising consultant Mark Rovner of the Carol/Trevelyan
Strategy Group told the *Chronicle of Philanthropy* recently, "The reality is the world is migrating online, and online giving is inevitably
going to follow. We're at a point now where it's not a matter of
whether the Internet will become the dominant small-gift platform,
it's just a matter of when" (Wallace, 2005). It's time for your school
to get in on the action.

STARTING A FUNDRAISING SITE

Schools and districts can leverage their Web sites to raise money in
a number of ways. For instance, they can include links to affiliate
sales programs connected to online retailers, such as Amazon.com,
and then reap a percentage of each sale when visitors click through
and buy.

They also can add appeals for individual fundraisers, such as
an alumni pledge challenge that pits classes against each other to

see which one can bring in the most donations. And they can provide updates on where donors' dollars are going while encouraging additional giving.

But the most plugged-in schools have gone well beyond such add-on initiatives to create robust sites completely dedicated to fundraising. Some solicit pledges, while others host online auctions.

With the help of Minnesota-based Lawson, the St. Paul and Minneapolis districts now share a Web site through which supporters can make direct credit card donations to any of their individual schools, the *Star Tribune* reported (Kimball, 2004). After taking out 3 percent of the donation amount to cover processing fees, the rest of the money collected through ImpactSchools.org goes right to the designated schools. Visitors can make contributions of $10 or more. They can even select which programs they want their money to support.

Software providers that offer fundraising products for schools and other nonprofit groups include Lawson (www.lawson.com); Blackbaud, Inc. (www.blackbaud.com); Convio (www.convio.com), which offers visitors a tip-filled *Online Fundraising Guide* for free download; and AuctionPay (www.auctionpay.com), which boasts that it has partnered with 4,000 schools and other nonprofit organizations and processed more than $400 million in donations and auction bids since 2002.

Another useful resource is the database of employers that match their workers' charitable donations at http://case.hep data.com. School foundations would do well to ask donors to check the database and see if they can get their contributions supersized.

BIDDING FOR DONORS ON EBAY

The eBay auction site provides another online fundraising avenue to schools. In fact, Menlo School in Atherton, California—where eBay CEO Meg Whitman sends her kids—helped start the trend of holding charity auctions on the site. The school's first such event raised about $6,000 through the sale of 75 items donated by parents and students, the *Los Angeles Times* reported (Alexander, 2004). Organizers of that fundraiser suggest soliciting donations of items that sell best at the site, such as sports equipment, musical instruments, electronics, and all kinds of collectibles.

PLAYING THE PERCENTAGES

Several online shopping portals kick back a percentage of the proceeds to schools when parents buy products after registering at their sites. Schoolpop.com, for instance, claims in its "Company Overview" that it has contributed more than $200 million to over 30,000 schools and other nonprofits nationwide through such purchases. Another popular site is eScrip.com.

PICKING UP PLEDGES

Fundable.org enables school groups to set up pages to collect online pledges toward a specific monetary goal within a set time frame. Donors only have their accounts charged when (and if) the goal is met. Fundable.org then passes the total on to the group, minus a 5 percent service fee.

TURNING TRASH INTO CASH

ClassroomClassifieds.com, an online garage sale benefiting education, invites schools to get in on the trash-to-treasure action. The site was launched by Maine's Falmouth Education Association, the *Portland Press Herald* reported (Nacelewicz, 2004). The concept is simple: people interested in selling their secondhand goods get free listings on the site in exchange for donating a portion of the sale to their local schools. Sellers have listed everything from handmade furniture to used cars. Schools pay as little as $20 a month to use the service.

DIGGING UP DONORSCHOOSE DOLLARS

An Interview With Charles Best

Back in 2000, Charles Best was teaching at Wings Academy, an alternative high school in the Bronx, New York, when he got the idea for a Web site where teachers could solicit donations for class projects. With help from his students, DonorsChoose.org soon was born. In 2005, the site won Amazon.com's Nonprofit

Innovation Award. So far, DonorsChoose has generated more than $8 million for projects that have touched 479,000-plus students in the cities and states it serves. Best, now the full-time DonorsChoose CEO, provides a peek at the site's expansion plans and tips for getting projects funded.

The site started with proposals posted by 11 of your colleagues. Six years later, you've generated some $8 million. Has word spread mainly by word of mouth?

Partly it's just teachers telling more of their teacher friends. It's also donors getting feedback packages—the thank-you letters and photographs that the classroom puts together for every donor—and deciding they're going to make another donation and tell all of their friends. Part of it is expansion to other parts of the country beyond New York City. And then much of it is thanks to media coverage and corporate sponsors.

You started in the Bronx, but didn't you expand first to one of the Carolinas?

North Carolina was the first region to which DonorsChoose expanded after New York City. We now serve all of the public schools in North and South Carolina, Texas, Louisiana, Mississippi, Alabama, and Indiana. We also serve the schools of Los Angeles, the San Francisco Bay Area, and Chicago.

Tell us more about the feedback packages classrooms send to donors?

We've been doing those thank-you letters and photographs from day one of DonorsChoose. People want the opportunity to choose exactly where their money will go, and it's a human urge to hear back from the recipients of one's generosity. So we saw the immediate appeal for donors. What has been really exciting has been to hear back from teachers. We've actually had a number of teachers who've had multiple projects funded tell us that their students' writing ability has improved as a result of writing so many thank-you notes. There is an extra level of motivation for students because, rather than a regular homework task, they're writing to a person who has delivered books to their classroom or enabled them to go on a field trip. So 99 percent of the time, students send thank-you notes that are just wonderfully sincere and well written. There's another educational piece to it: students are part of the philanthropy. Something is expected of them. The students are actually vital to DonorsChoose. It's their thank-you notes that inspire further contributions.

What types of projects work best at DonorsChoose?

Our donors often pay attention to the school's free lunch rate, which is listed beside every proposal. Many donors want to give where there is the most economic need. So they are likelier to fund a proposal at a school with a 50 percent free lunch rate rather than at one with a 5 percent rate. Other than that, all we can really say is that proposals that cost under $500 are funded more quickly. No surprise there. We can also give teachers the encouraging advice that experience with grant writing is not a requirement. People reading teacher proposals at DonorsChoose are ordinary folks who prefer to read plainspoken, from-the-heart compositions. And so jargon and technical writing is discouraged. We encourage teachers to speak from the heart about a student experience and to paint a mental picture for the donor of what student learning is going to take place if a given resource is funded.

Do you have a minimum dollar amount that you like to have people ask for?

We'd like to see a proposal for $100 or more just because of the labor that DonorsChoose is going to put into authenticating the proposal, purchasing the materials for the teacher, having them shipped to the classroom, and developing these photographs. It becomes somewhat inefficient if we're expending that labor on resources that are less than $100.

What's the most expensive project you've seen filled?

There was a South Bronx kindergarten teacher who couldn't take her students out to recess because the playground was in such disrepair. And just to vent her frustration, she went to DonorsChoose and submitted a proposal for a new $20,000 playground. We thought she was nuts. But she clearly explained how students would benefit if the playground was provided, and she did identify a $20,000 prefabricated playground. Three weeks later, it was fully funded by a wealthy couple in Manhattan.

Do you allow incremental donations so that multiple people can fund big projects?

Our motto is citizen philanthropy. We let somebody with $10 be a philanthropist. And even if you gave the first 10 bucks on a $1,000 proposal, you would still get an e-mail addressed to you from the teacher, thanking you for the project that you've helped bring to life. Everybody gets an e-mailed thank-you note from the teacher personally addressed to them. And those who complete the project get the hard-copy feedback package.

Have you had any fraud problems?

We once had a $50,000 culinary field trip to France and Israel proposed. It was justified in one paragraph. And we had a photography field trip to Cuba on which only the teacher would be going. Those proposals never saw the light of day. DonorsChoose is open just to public school teachers. We define "public school" expansively and include charter schools, prison schools, Department of Defense schools, and Bureau of Indian Affairs schools. But when teachers who don't fall within that broad definition of public schools submit a proposal, we have to turn them back. And that's really what most of the vetting process is for. Because a teacher does not receive cash via DonorsChoose, there's not a whole lot of incentive to even try to commit fraud.

You're basically a fulfillment service as well, taking the cash and turning it into the items. That's a labor-intensive process. Is that why you roll out new offices gradually?

That is why our expansion has been gradual, but over the last five years, we've been developing technology to automate and streamline that back-end labor. As a nonprofit, we pioneered the use of a procurement technology, which has automated the verification and purchase of materials. What used to take us an hour now takes us a minute or two. So with technology like that, we are positioning ourselves well and looking to raise the funds to open across the United States to every public school in the country by fall of 2007.

You have a central oversight office that you run in Manhattan. And then there are regional offices. Is that how it's set up?

Yes, there tend to be one- or two-person regional offices. Their job ranges from teacher outreach to donor outreach, to forging strategic partnerships with local corporations, to public speaking, to media outreach. They're basically the ones who are responsible for the success of DonorsChoose in their regions.

How many people overall do you have working for the operation now?

All included—regional staff, national, front-end, and back-end—we are a team now of 25. Most of the 16,000 projects that have been funded by our Web site were fulfilled when our staff was 2 or 5 or 10. We've only just hit a staff of 25. So we have managed to stay pretty lean.

How do you fund your operational expenses?

At DonorsChoose, if you click to fund a $100 class set of *Hamlet,* you have two options. The first option lets you say, "I want 100 percent of my donation going only to the purchase of this set of *Hamlet.*" And you're still going to get the photographs and thank-you letters. But a second option invites you to include a 15 percent cost of fulfillment for the work that we perform. And 90 percent of our donors choose to underwrite the fulfillment. Revenue thus generated makes us, bit by bit, more and more self-sustaining. It's kind of a nice moral that if you present it in a transparent and optional way, then donors want to help you out with your overhead.

What are the average and median donation levels from visitors?

The average is about $200, but that is skewed upward by the large gifts that we have received and by sponsorships. The median might be lower, because more than 50 percent of our donors have average household incomes under $100,000. So it really is a model of citizen philanthropy. There are huge numbers of working-class and middle-class folks who use our site because it is the one place where, with 10 bucks, they've got the same choice and accountability and feedback from the recipients that Bill Gates gets from a million-dollar gift.

What's the average number of projects a teacher gets funded?

It's not so much a "one-and-out" situation as it is a "one-and-hooked." Half of our teachers have had 2 or more projects funded, and then there are 200 teachers who have had more than 10 projects funded each. Overall, 9,000 teachers are using our site, and roughly 7,000 of them have been successful.

Is there a time limit on each proposal?

Proposals have an eight-month shelf life. Two-thirds of them are funded. There's a 65 percent success rate, and most proposals under $500 are funded within two or three months. People sometimes ask whether teachers are disappointed, but it's more like surprised celebration when they are funded. At two-thirds funded, the success rate far exceeds what you see from the traditional grant process.

You've already had donations from all 50 states and 11 foreign countries. Who are your average donors? Are they retired teachers or still in education, for instance?

The vast majority are women. The bare majority do not have children. And a good number are current educators or former educators. The donor profile is of a person who cares more about choosing where their money is going to go, seeing the impact, and having a chance to get personally involved in their philanthropy than it is about education or schools.

Anything else that teachers and administrators should know?

Although every DonorsChoose proposal involves a request for materials or for a resource or a field trip, each proposal needs to focus on the student experience that's going to take place if a given material is provided. That's one piece of advice we always come back to.

SOURCE: Telephone interview with Charles Best, September 20, 2006.

GETTING SCHOOL SUPPLY WISHES GRANTED

An Interview With Classroom Wishlist Founder Craig Harmer

After a career as an Internet strategist in California's Silicon Valley, Craig Harmer decided to quit the high-tech rat race a few years back and devote himself to making a positive difference in the lives of teachers. One of his sisters, an elementary reading teacher, had died of lung cancer, and he wanted to do something meaningful in her memory. That's how Classroom Wishlist was born. The San Jose, California-based nonprofit helps teachers around the nation solicit donations for needed supplies. Less than a year after launching in July of 2005, the site had registered more than 14,000 teachers and shipped supplies to all 50 states.

What gave you the idea for the site?

About five years ago, my daughter was in eighth grade and came home with the wish list that teachers send home at the beginning of every year. And it had on it, among other things, five boxes of Kleenex. My wife, who's a nurse, sent back the Kleenexes. And when we go to parent-teacher night, we also always take care of anything that didn't get covered on their list. So we went to parent-teacher night a couple weeks later, and we asked the teacher what didn't get covered. She kind of smiled, then walked over to the closet and opened it up. There were 25 boxes of Kleenex and no pencils. Here we are in the heart of Silicon Valley and I'd been doing Internet strategy for these big high-tech companies, and it was frustrating for me that teachers couldn't utilize the same technology to get what they needed and wanted.

Those notes aren't a very efficient way to do it?

No, and teachers still do it all over. And they don't get what they need, so they end up going out-of-pocket for it.

Give us a thumbnail sketch of how to log on and participate?

It's a three-step process. Go to http://classroomwishlist.org and register as a teacher. We have a look-up table so you can find your school, etc. And then you create your wish list. We have a catalog of about 120,000 different items—everything from PCs to pencils, different book titles, art supplies, band supplies, garden supplies, office supplies, you name it. The third step is for teachers to make the list a point of focus in their communications with parents by sending home fliers about it, bringing it up at parent-teacher night, putting it on the classroom Web site, and involving the PTA. It's all about motivating parents to go online.

Some of the teachers are asking for big-ticket items like digital projectors. Can you give some guidelines to educators about what they're most likely to get funded?

Funny you should ask that. I recently visited a local teacher. She had gone onto the site and built a wish list with about a dozen items. Many of them were less than $50. But she had three $150 bookcases on there. The thing that breeds the most success, we have found, is that on the site, there's a customized flier the teacher can send home with the kids or that the PTA can send home on behalf of the teachers. If that happens, we have found that the parents step up. This teacher sent home the flier, and every item on her wish list that was less than $30 got taken care of, along with a couple of things between $30 and $50. Nobody touched the bookcases, even though we allow partial donations for the bigger items.

One of my favorite stories is about a teacher out of New York who didn't have a whiteboard in her classroom. And she listed a $300 whiteboard. Within two weeks, parents, friends, her parents, and the teacher all donated $5 to $20 at a time, and they got her whiteboard. So we do accept partial donations on the bigger items. But we've found that most parents want to say, "I donated something, and you got this thing from me," not, "I donated a 50th of your whiteboard."

We had a teacher in Arizona who put, among other things, a package of star stickers on her wish list for $1.70. And we had a parent who went in and donated $1.70 to get her those gold stars. What that $1.70 has done is it allowed the parent to be involved, it allowed the teacher to get those gold stars, and it allowed the teacher to reward the kids.

What kind of overhead are you looking at to do these transactions?
We're getting about 35 percent discounts from most of our vendors. Of that 35 percent, 15 of it on average goes directly to the donor, so the stuff that we have out there is discounted 15 percent off of retail. Of the remaining 20 percent, we take 10 for our overhead. The other 10 percent we use to fund the wish lists of Title 1 schools that can't afford to fund their own lists.

Designating 10 percent for Title 1 schools is a progressive approach. Were you concerned about the funding disparity issue?
Absolutely. One of my sisters teaches in a Title 1 school, and they are right next to a district in Utah that is really well funded while they're not. Initially, I had people get after me because we were allowing private schools to build wish lists. But some of the private

schools have items on their lists in the $4,000–$5,000 range. I said, "I am tickled pink if I can get a private school to come in and have the parents do $100,000 in donations for their stuff, because that's $10,000 I can use to fund Title I schools."

Because rich schools are going to do the fundraising whether your site exists or not?

Yes. And by using the 10 percent, we're doing some redistribution to poorer schools.

With DonorsChoose, you have philanthropic folks from Nebraska funding school projects in Florida. It sounds like you're seeing this more as a way to facilitate parents to help in their schools. But do you see any of that kind of philanthropy where someone logs on and funds a project they have no connection to?

After the hurricanes [in 2005], I bet we had a hundred donations from around the nation into Texas, Mississippi, and Louisiana. We had a PTA from Minnesota that was trying to work through the National Education Association and its philanthropy site to do some stuff down in Louisiana, but they couldn't do it. So they went onto our site and adopted a school and took care of a whole bunch of stuff. The Texas schools we worked with were not hit by a hurricane; they were hit by the evacuees. So we saw teachers who went from 20 students in their classroom to 40. And they just didn't have the materials or budget to deal with the increase.

DonorsChoose focuses on having teachers send pictures of projects back to donors. Do you encourage sending thank-you notes, etc.?

DonorsChoose requires teachers to write a grant. I didn't want teachers to have to write a grant to get pencils into their classrooms. So on the basic supplies, no, we don't push that. But we do allow the teachers to see who made the donation and their e-mail address, unless the donor chooses to remain anonymous, and we encourage teachers to write notes back to their donors and let them know how much they appreciate them. We had one anonymous donor who donated some stuff, and as a result I got a package of about 30 pictures from this kindergarten class in Maine with a request to forward it off to the donor. The teacher had her class draw pictures thanking the donor for the stuff.

Are you looking to develop a corporate wing for ongoing donations in addition to your initial angel investors?

We're calling them and e-mailing them. And we're also looking at ways to help local PTAs and schools reach out to their business communities and find partners.

What's the latest innovation on the site?

One feature we recently added is supply lists, where teachers can build lists of supplies their students need to bring at the beginning of the year, and the parents can go to the site and click "buy one of these lists." And 5 percent of the supply list cost goes back to the PTA of the school for their fundraising efforts. The week before school starts, we ship the supply lists to the teachers. We also allow the teachers to subsidize up to 10 percent of the classroom if they have a couple of kids who are not going to be able to afford everything on the supply list. That way, everybody has equal footing when they come through the door.

What will it take for your site to reach critical mass and become self-sustaining?

To do it right, we need 62 schools to be fully engaged. That means every teacher fully getting all their stuff through it.

What is your goal with this looking down the road five years?

In the next five years, we would like to see every school in the nation at least have awareness about Classroom Wishlist and have the opportunity to participate. There's no reason that structurally, architecturally, we can't handle that. Ideally, we would like to see the $500 or $600 teachers spend every year out-of-pocket distributed so that parents of each of the 30 students in the classroom spend $20. Teachers can afford $600 a lot less than each of those parents could afford $20. If we can fund those real needs in the classroom and distribute the burden across the classroom, we'd be really excited about that.

SOURCE: Telephone interview with Craig Harmer, March 1, 2006.

CHAPTER FOUR

The Publicity Payoff

How to Generate Positive Press for Your FUNdraiser

Newspapers and local TV newscasts hunger to tell positive stories about schools in the communities they cover. Unfortunately, simply doing the things you're supposed to be doing—keeping a lid on school crime, delivering steady gains in test scores, and generally turning out competent students— usually won't grab headlines. But if you can provide reporters with a "hook," or an out-of-the-ordinary context in which to nestle those success stories, you'll soon generate positive press.

Creative and educational fundraisers make great story hooks. They couple fun, highly visual events with stories that enable reporters to point out real school needs even while telling feel-good stories about dedicated educators, parents, and students going the extra mile to cover financial shortfalls and provide worthwhile extras.

Even so, newsrooms are busy, understaffed places—much like schools—and even these great stories can fall through the cracks. Increase the likelihood that your school will earn the positive coverage it deserves by taking the following steps to promote your fundraiser to the media.

1. Launch an internal media blitz. Start your campaign by reaching out to parents and other members of the school community with the media you produce in-house. Provide regular updates about fundraising activities in school newsletters, both in print and online. Create a countdown page on your school's Web site so members of the community can follow along as you strive to meet financial goals. Send information to the district communications office for inclusion in its publications. Not only will these stories keep parents and others informed about the fundraising situation, they will serve as stealth press releases as well. Beat reporters regularly comb through newsletters produced by the organizations they cover for story tips.

2. Release information in a timely manner. Don't wait until the day of the fundraiser to let reporters know about it. But don't send out a press release announcing a spring event when school starts in the fall, either. Properly timing your press outreach will greatly increase your chances of getting the fundraiser covered. Start by sending out a detailed press release about a week before the big event. Then phone, fax, or e-mail a reminder the day before the fundraiser kicks off. Send the press release home to parents on the same day you mail it to editors and reporters. Doing so will generate additional excitement about the event, remind parents to pitch in, and alert them to watch for coverage in the local media. Many parents also appreciate receiving a heads-up that the press has been invited to campus.

3. Get personal. Don't address your press release to the generic "editor" at the local paper. Find out which reporter covers your school and send the release directly to that person's attention. When it comes to generating local TV news coverage, find out the name of the station's assignment editor and address releases to that person. Because fundraisers often provide compelling visuals, you also should address a separate release to the photo editor of the newspaper. You might well get coverage in the form of a section-leading photo with an extended caption that hits the highlights of the event. And more people will read that caption than any story buried inside the paper.

To have a great shot at gaining coverage, all you need is a compelling story idea sent to the right person. But it never hurts to establish rapport with local education reporters even before sending that first press release. One way to do that is to meet them for a one-on-one, get-to-know-you cup of coffee. Another nice gesture: If they report something well, drop them an e-mail or personal note complimenting their work. Journalists tend to be a bit suspicious of praise coming from people they might cover, but offering genuine (and occasional) kudos can help establish a good working relationship.

4. Make yourself available. Share as much contact information for yourself as possible in the press release—including an e-mail address along with direct office and cell phone numbers, if possible. It's unfair, but reporters spike many optional stories when they can't reach sources on the first attempt.

5. The devil's in the details. Make sure each press release includes the time, date, and place of the fundraiser as well as information about exactly how the money will be used. (Drafting a complete and accurate press release can even help you discover any last-minute holes in the event plan.) If there's an educational component to the event, so much the better. And remember, journalists tend to love anniversaries, so you can increase the chances a long-time fundraiser will gain some coverage if it's the 5th, 10th, 25th, or 50th annual iteration of the event.

ADDED ATTRACTION

Ⓢ For general insights into crafting effective school publicity campaigns, download the free guide *Raising the Bar for School PR: New Standards for the School Public Relations Profession* at www.nspra.org/StandardsBooklet.pdf.

SAMPLE PRESS RELEASE

**NAME OF SCHOOL gets creative to
raise funds for WORTHY GOAL**

DATE

For Immediate Release

CONTACT INFORMATION

NAME OF SCHOOL will host NAME OF EVENT to raise funds for NAME OF WORTHY GOAL at TIME, DATE, & PLACE. ADD INFORMATION ABOUT TICKET PRICES, REFRESHMENTS TO BE SERVED, AND ANY OTHER IMPORTANT DETAILS HERE.

In addition to bringing the school community closer together, this fundraiser has a creative, educational component as well. It will help students OUTLINE EDUCATIONAL IMPACT even as they help raise money for REITERATE WORTHY GOAL.

"PITHY QUOTE," says PRINCIPAL NAME.

Part II

50 FUNdraising Ideas

Rake in the Bucks With These Creative Concepts

CHAPTER FIVE

Excellent Extravaganzas

NO. 1

Educational Film Festival

Screen a series of unintentionally hilarious educational movies from bygone eras.

Funding Sources: Ticket sales, concession sales, sponsorships

Potential Haul: < $1,000

Possible Partners/Sponsors: Movie theaters, video stores

SUCCESS SNAPSHOT

- Raid your school's old audiovisual closet for choice filmstrips and educational films from the 1950s and 1960s. Craft campy fliers and press releases designed to attract nostalgic adults and ironic teens to attend a festival featuring films on everything from maintaining proper hygiene to ducking and covering one's way out of a nuclear attack. On the big night, deck out ticket takers in classic nerd glasses and array A/V carts, filmstrip projectors, and overhead projectors throughout the lobby. Enlist a presenter to don a white lab coat and introduce the entries in a way that would make Dr. Frank Baxter from those old Bell Science films proud. Speaking of which, here's a fun fact: the first three films in the Bell Science series were directed by none other than Frank Capra, starting with *Our Mr. Sun* in 1956 and followed by *Hemo the Magnificent* (which focuses on the circulatory system) and *The Strange Case of the Cosmic Rays*. Think about that the next time you watch *It's a Wonderful Life* or *Mr. Smith Goes to Washington*.

ADDED ATTRACTIONS

$ If you can't find any dusty old classroom films to screen, seek out providers on the Web. One of the best known outfits is A/V Geeks, which boasts an archive of more than 18,000 educational and industrial films, including such gems as *Squeak the Squirrel* and *Soapy the Germ Fighter*. The Geeks sell inexpensive thematic collections of educational film shorts on DVD and VHS. Peruse the titles and watch free streaming previews at www.avgeeks.com.

$ For even more information on the history of educational films, visit the Academic Film Archive of North America at www.afana.org.

$ Increase student involvement by enlisting teens to create an educational film parody that can be shown at the festival.

NO. 2

Inspiring Expositions

Put on an "inspiration expo" replete with local experts on fascinating subjects.

Funding Sources: Ticket sales, concession sales, sponsorships, exhibitor fees

Potential Haul: > $5,000

Possible Partners/Sponsors: Speaker's bureaus, colleges, universities, civic groups

SUCCESS SNAPSHOT

⑤ Workshops on topics as varied as songwriting and crime scene investigations were on tap at the Inspiration Expo produced by Currey Ingram Academy in Brentwood, Tennessee, the *Tennessean* reported (Garton, 2006). The private school reached out to parents and other community members to serve as expert presenters for the day-long event, which raised money for the art, music, and drama programs through an admission fee ($10 for adults, $5 for Grades K–5 students) and a silent auction. The inaugural expo in 2006 boasted seven hours of programming, including shark tales from a maker of underwater documentaries; songwriting advice from the man who wrote the hit "Maniac" from *Flashdance*; a "*CSI* for Real!" workshop led by a forensic investigator; a breakfast talk by children's book author and illustrator Peter Reynolds; garden design tips from a noted local gardener; an inspirational speech from a player with the NFL's Tennessee Titans; and technology-themed how-to sessions on blogging, podcasting, and digital photography. "We wanted to have an event that would celebrate the creativity and imagination we see so much in the children," said the president of the academy's parent organization. "Enrichment is oftentimes what our students really excel at, so this is a way of celebrating our talents." Officials hoped to turn the expo into Currey Ingram's main annual fundraiser. "We knew we wanted something that went hand-in-hand with the mission of our school," said the director of school advancement. "We hope people will learn something and might be inspired to be creative in their own interests."

NO. 3

Auctioning Experiences

Build buzz for silent and live auctions by letting folks bid on amazing outings.

Funding Sources: Ticket sales, auction proceeds, sponsorships

Potential Haul: > $5,000

Possible Partners/Sponsors: Auction houses, corporate donors

SUCCESS SNAPSHOTS

⑤ Increase the chances of scoring media coverage for school auctions while heightening the excitement among attendees by opening up bids on a few truly remarkable outings. As *Crain's Chicago Business* (Bertagnoli, 2006) noted recently, "Experiences are the hot 'going, going, gone' items at charity auctions these days." The added "wow" factor likely will create a halo effect that boosts the bidding on nice-but-not-noteworthy items as well. Chicago-area charities, for instance, have had success in the past few years auctioning off walk-on film roles; lunches with B-list celebrities, such as Kathie Lee Gifford and Pat O'Brien; and meetings with A-list politicians, such as Senator Barack Obama. Other popular prizes included trips to a Wyoming dinosaur dig and a "fashion week" in Manhattan, onstage appearances with rock bands, posing sessions with top photographers, and in-home cooking parties led by catering firms. "Charities make more money with intangibles" because such experiences can be otherwise impossible for the general public to secure, said Leslie Hindman of Leslie Hindman Auctioneers. And as one auction organizer put it, "People want what nobody else has."

⑤ Cool school-related experiences helped Tennessee's Riverdale Elementary rake in $12,000 from about 500 attendees during an auction of prize-packed baskets, the *Commercial Appeal* reported (Womack, 2004). Some of the containers were filled with donated items from local businesses; those were dubbed Power of Partnership baskets. But each homeroom in the school also put together a themed basket for auction. Those included a teacher-hosted slumber party for three girls complete with some makeover fun, lunch and a movie with a first-grade instructor, and the opportunity for two students to take on the role of principal for half a day each. Bids for the most popular baskets were in the $200–$230 range, making the splurges more affordable than those offered by some school auctions.

⑤ Brookside School in Bloomfield Hills, Michigan, stimulated auction interest by offering a "*Top Gun* experience" that gave winning bidders the chance to try their hands at simulated aerial combat while copiloting a Marchetti aircraft trainer, the *Detroit News* reported (Pope, 2005). The prize, popular at local charity auctions, typically brings in

$3,500–$4,500 per participant. Another area event snared $6,000 for a package that included a trip to New York City to meet Joel Grey and see one of his Broadway shows. The man who put together both prizes, auctioneer Dan Stall, suggested that event organizers should think six degrees of separation, asking school supporters for contacts that could land them celebrity lunch dates and other exciting outings. "Everyone knows somebody who knows somebody," Stall noted.

⑤ In Texas, the Carroll Independent School District has been auctioning experience packages for so many years that topping previous efforts can be a real challenge, the *Dallas Morning News* reported (Fox, 2005). Previous outings have included a chartered jet to a World Series game, a trip to see *The Ellen DeGeneres Show*, and a two-year Lexus lease. In 2004, the dinner auction sold out all 1,000 seats at $100 each and brought in $284,000 for the district's education foundation. "There are always other events like this out there raising money, and you have to find ways to stand out," said the foundation's executive director.

⑤ Elite private schools in Southern California often tap into entertainment industry ties to come up with eye-popping auction items, such as a cameo in a Will Ferrell film, sports lessons from a professional athlete, tickets to an *American Idol* finale, or even an in-home meal whipped up by celebrity chef Wolfgang Puck, the *Los Angeles Times* reported (Rivera, 2006). The good news is that even those auctions feature popular packages that schools in other areas can put together easily. "Vacation, jewelry, sporting events, entertainment, and teacher outings are some of the biggest sellers," said one event organizer, who added that it's important to focus on assembling an array of items diverse enough to provide something fun for everyone in attendance.

⑤ Public schools with great academic reputations can sometimes use a simple marketing hook to entice big fundraising auction bids: "For less than you'd pay for private school tuition, you can support our educational mission and go home with a great prize, too." A recent PTA auction for New York City's P.S. 87 provided a perfect example of that pitch in action, the *New York Sun* reported (Kolben, 2006). The event's headline-grabbing item was an afternoon tea with actress Ashley Olsen, of the Olsen twins fame. The mother who won the prize for her young daughter with a $5,000 bid said, "The way we look at it, it's our donation to the school for the year. We feel like our kids are getting a great education there, and we don't pay for private school." Now there's a great way to sell an auction to public school parents.

NO. 4
Double the Auction Fun

When a bidder wins the hottest auction item, wow the crowd by putting up an extra one for sale.

Funding Sources: Ticket sales, auction proceeds, sponsorships

Potential Haul: > $5,000

Possible Partners/Sponsors: Corporate donors, auction houses

SUCCESS SNAPSHOT

⑤ What's better than offering up a thrilling, one-of-a-kind centerpiece item at a school auction? Why, pulling a second one out of your hat, of course. That was the smart strategy employed recently by Stanley Clark School in South Bend, Indiana ("Rollin' in the Dough," 2006). After selling off a guitar autographed by members of the Rolling Stones for $20,000, the headmaster stunned—and, more important, delighted—the crowd by bringing forth a second one for auction. Another frenzied round of bidding ensued—as did an additional $20,000 sale. To make sure there were no hard feelings, the first winning bidder got his pick of the autographed axes.

ADDED ATTRACTION

- Ⓢ Why not try for a triple hit of publicity by auctioning off a package that combines a wild experience, a big celebrity, and a truly unusual item?

NO. 5

Housing Markets

Host home tours with a twist.

Funding Sources: Ticket sales, sponsorships

Potential Haul: > $5,000

Possible Partners/Sponsors: Real estate brokers, developers, homeowners' associations, historical societies, home improvement stores

SUCCESS SNAPSHOTS

- Ⓢ Helping to feed the huge public appetite for home improvement tips, California's Moraga Women's Society threw a homes tour for local schools, libraries, and parks that featured only newly remodeled houses, the *Contra Costa Times* reported (De Jesus, 2005). "We really like to get remodels because so many people are interested in remodeling these days and they can get ideas from these homes," one organizer said. Added another, "People just love to see how homes are decorated and see how they can bring their own homes up-to-date."
- Ⓢ People who go all out on holiday decorations seem naturally inclined to share the good cheer with others. A cancer support organization in California's San Fernando Valley taps into that spirit by throwing an Annual Holiday Homes Tour

featuring the area's most elaborately (yet tastefully) decorated houses, the *Daily News of Los Angeles* reported (Sodders, 2005). The self-guided event, which started in the early 1990s, brings in up to $100,000 for The Wellness Community as it plays host to some 4,000 locals over a December weekend. Participating homeowners tend to create thematic displays, such as a "winter wonderland" combining Christmas and Hanukkah accents. "It gives you that warm feeling of childhood," one visitor said. "Things are so rushed and artificial now. When we decorate for the holidays, it makes people relax."

⑤ A home tour for a Palm Springs, California, children's museum really went to the dogs—by featuring designer "canine casitas" at every house on the fundraiser's route. The fancy doghouses, such as the "pooch palace" palapa, were then sold at a silent auction that capped off the tour ("In the Doghouse," 2006).

⑤ An Edible Art Tour of 29 local galleries raised money for school arts programs in Santa Fe, New Mexico, as part of the ARTfeast event put on by a nonprofit group called ArtSmart, the *Santa Fe New Mexican* reported (Cook-Romero, 2006). Area restaurants catered hors d'oeuvres at each location, so those who purchased $30 tickets could munch their way through as many galleries as they wished during the three-hour event. The festival, which also includes an art-themed homes tour, brings in about $60,000 a year. In 2006, organizers enlisted the city's fifth- and sixth-graders to enter a plate-design competition. Sixty finalists were chosen by local art teachers from more than 1,000 entries. The students then used their entries to decorate ceramic plates at a paint-your-own-pottery shop. Each child crafted two plates—one to keep and one to auction off. The designs also were featured on that year's event poster.

⑤ Rather than focus on the older restorations often featured on home tours, Chapman Elementary in Portland, Oregon, decided to showcase midcentury properties in what was the city's first tour of modern homes, the *Daily Journal of Commerce* reported (Ryan, 2006). The event was so popular, it sold out for all 45 days of its run, prompting fans of modern architecture to post pleas for spare tickets online. One real estate agent predicted that such tours would do well in cities across the nation. "There's always been interest" in modern homes, he said. "The interest just seems to have gotten a lot bigger over the past few years."

⑨ Garden tours can get a big buzz going if they employ memorable themes. One recent spring in the San Francisco Bay Area saw fundraisers focused on "secret gardens," "hidden gardens," repositories of native plants, and butterfly gardens, *Inside Bay Area* reported (Jardina, 2006). And proving that all good parties end up in the kitchen, the Heart of the Home Kitchen Tour was another popular fundraiser there.

⑨ Forget houses. A community service group in Jefferson, Iowa, recently drove off with a nice stash of cash by holding a five-hour tour of noteworthy local garages, the *Des Moines Register* reported (Challender, 2006). Of the eight garages on the circuit, one looked like an old barn, several displayed antique vehicles, and another showcased nifty storage systems. It was an idea with special appeal to the men of the community, one organizer said. "That's why we put it on Father's Day weekend."

NO. 6

Pampering Moms

Give the women of the school community a well-deserved break for fun and games.

Funding Sources: Ticket sales, concession sales, product sales, exhibitor fees

Potential Haul: > $5,000

Possible Partners/Sponsors: Corporate donors, women's groups

SUCCESS SNAPSHOTS

⑤ "Girls' night out" was the theme of a fun fair that attracted women of all ages to California's Tulare Youth Center, the *Fresno Bee* reported (Avila, 2006)—and the watchwords were *pampering* and *fun*. Organizers quickly sold out all 300 tickets for the event and estimated they could have sold 200 more. Attendees enjoyed chocolate fondue while moving from booth to booth for makeup advice, hairdo makeovers, light jewelry and accessories shopping, and tips on topics ranging from finding the best brassiere fit to crafting lovely floral arrangements. The evening also included a silent auction of items with multi-generational appeal. "This was great. It gave me a chance to be with my daughter," said one mom, who brought her 10-year-old. "And the way the schedule is—busy, busy, busy—this was the perfect way for us to spend some good, quality time together." This is an excellent example of a fundraiser that gives back, in terms of enjoyment, as much as it takes in.

⑤ A Christmas in July initiative to raise holiday funds for underprivileged children in Seminole, Florida, treated residents to such spa services as manicures, massages, mini-facials, and haircuts for $10 a pop, the *St. Petersburg Times* reported (Lykins, 2006). The three-hour event, dubbed Cutting for a Cause, was organized by a local women's club in partnership with a salon whose workers donated their services. No appointments were accepted; instead, customers were seated on a first-come, first-served basis. The plan was to make a big difference in the lives of little kids. "We send out letters to school guidance counselors and seek their help in identifying families and children that have special needs during the holidays," one organizer said. "We're thinking it will be a good time for kids to come in and get a nice haircut before school, and, hey, where can you get a spa haircut for $10? It's a great deal."

⑤ Adult women reconnected with some fond childhood experiences when they attended the PJ's With a Purpose fundraiser in Lake Worth, Florida, the *Palm Beach Post* reported (Rodgers, 2005). They paid $125 each to show up at the Gulfstream Hotel in their pajamas and engage in slumber party mainstays, such as manicures, makeovers, psychic readings, and dance lessons, while chowing down on decadent food. Organizers even held hula hoop and dance contests at the benefit for a local legal aid society. For an extra $125 a head, attendees could opt to stay overnight and swap secrets until dawn.

❂ It was Mom's Night Out in DeSoto County, Mississippi, recently thanks to the PTO at Hernando Elementary. The four-and-a-half-hour shindig featured food and presentations by local representatives of Pampered Chef, Southern Living, and other in-home merchandise peddlers. "We want to draw attention to the stay-at-home moms that are starting their own businesses in order to spend more time with their children" ("Hernando PTO," 2006), the coordinator said. Meanwhile, the PTO for Academy Avenue Primary School in Weymouth, Massachusetts, charged guests $30 to attend Girls' Night Out complete with wine tastings, psychic readings, and salon services, the *Boston Globe* reported (Vaishnav, 2004).

NO. 7

Digging for Diamonds

A sandbox full of jewelry makes for glitzy, gritty fun.

Funding Sources: Raffle sales, sponsorships

Potential Haul: $1,000–$5,000

Possible Partners/Sponsors: Jewelers

SUCCESS SNAPSHOTS

❂ Here's the scoop on a jewel of an event: the Chattanooga Bar Auxiliary raised cash for a Tennessee children's shelter by giving donors the chance to scoop out a sandbox and win a diamond ring and other pieces of jewelry. Different pebbles represented different prizes, and attendees got to sift through three scoops of sand for $10, the *Chattanooga Times Free Press* reported (Siskin, 2000). When one man hit pay dirt with his second round of scoops, "you could hear his wife's squeals of joy throughout the galleries," one organizer said. The treasure hunt was the centerpiece of an auction and shopping evening.

⑨ A Tulsa, Oklahoma, Diamond Dig raised money for crime prevention programs by selling $5 scoops of sand from a large container stocked with several dozen loose gems and a half-carat diamond ("Jeweler," 1999). The host jewelry store also donated 5 percent of the proceeds from all sales during the event. Meanwhile, a Florida hospice threw a Digging for Diamonds evening, during which guests chipped in $1 a scoop to empty a sand trough of diamonds and other stones, the *Orlando Sentinel* reported (Pedicini, 1993).

NO. 8
Tea Partying

Leaf through these rich and tasty themes.

Funding Sources: Ticket sales, sponsorships

Potential Haul: $1,000–$5,000

Possible Partners/Sponsors: Restaurants, tearooms

SUCCESS SNAPSHOTS

⑨ Educational and charitable organizations around Macomb County, Michigan, regularly hold elegant tea party fundraisers, the *Detroit Free Press* reported (Jackson, 2006). Recent events have included Mother-Daughter Tea, Victorian Tea, Vintage Fashion Show Tea, Children's Victorian Tea Party, Victoria Day Tea, Easter Tea, Mother's Day Tea, Valentine's Tea, and Titanic Tea. That last one went well beyond the usual finger sandwiches and cakes, serving food from the doomed ocean liner's menu and giving guests boarding passes with information on passengers they would be portraying. (Organizations in other cities have hosted Titanic-themed dinner fundraisers featuring similarly fascinating journeys into history.) Why are tea parties enjoying a revival? "There's no technology involved," suggested one organizer. "Life is more relaxed."

⑨ Dollies dolled up in their best dresses proved a highlight of the Mother, Daughter, and Doll Tea Party fundraiser for Richland Academy in Mansfield, Ohio, the *Mansfield News Journal* reported (Whitmire, 2006). During the Saturday afternoon affair, the dolls were treated to hairdos by cosmetology students, who also painted the fingernails of their young owners. The lunch featured an American Girl doll raffle as well.

NO. 9
Dance Fever

Relive high school memories with an adult prom.

Funding Sources: Ticket sales, pledges, concession sales, sponsorships

Potential Haul: > $5,000

Possible Partners/Sponsors: Corporate donors, restaurants, formal wear shops, civic groups

SUCCESS SNAPSHOTS

⑨ Starry Night Prom, a benefit for Community Youth Development in Sarasota, Florida, annually draws about 200 adults set on revisiting the teen tradition and creating some good new memories, the *Sarasota Herald-Tribune* reported (Nagata, 2006). The event raises some $20,000 a year. Area high school students serve as chaperones, naturally, and the evening includes dinner, drinks, and a silent auction along with dancing and the election of a prom court. Lending credence to the notion that youth may be wasted on the young, many attendees report having a more enjoyable, relaxed time at the adult prom than they did in high school. But they have teens to thank for their good time—students came up with the fundraiser when they saw how interested their parents were in their children's prom nights. "It's a positive partnership between kids and adults," one young chaperone said.

⑤ Here's a great way to throw an adult prom fundraiser on a tight budget: hold it the night after the regular prom and use the same theme and decorations. That's what organizers did in Hatton, North Dakota, recently, piggybacking on Hatton High's *Aladdin*-themed prom ("Prom Fund-Raiser," 2006). The event was alcohol-free so that under-21 residents could attend, and it included a grand march and hors d'oeuvres along with dancing. Tickets went for $15 each or $25 per couple.

⑤ Need some good marketing hooks for an adult prom? The organizers of one such fundraiser in Shelby County, Indiana, shared several with the *Indianapolis Star* (McDaniel, 2004). For one thing, attendees don't have to stress out about whether they're going to be asked. "The best thing about the evening is that this time you will know for sure you are going and who you are going with," one organizer noted. Another cited the lack of a curfew as a plus. Added a third, "I get to pick out my dress. My mom did it last time." The county's chamber of commerce launched its adult prom in 2004 with a "moonlight on Main Street" theme, a DJ spinning hits from the 1950s and beyond, appetizers, and a specialty drink dubbed the "moondew." Other smart moves included enlisting two other groups to provide support services as their own minifundraisers: the local Kiwanis Club handled valet parking duties, and a college sorority ran the coat check. Retired teachers were enlisted as chaperones, and the evening included a screening of a video history of county schools. "It is a walking yearbook of still photos," an organizer noted. "We will have lots of yearbooks from Shelbyville and area schools on display, too." Talk about a moonlit stroll down memory lane!

ADDED ATTRACTIONS

- Ⓢ Some adult proms add a pledge drive component that bestows the king and queen designation on the biggest fundraisers.
- Ⓢ You also could host a backwards prom, or "morp." After a service learning project raised $5,000 to sponsor a child through the Make-A-Wish Foundation, students at Schilling Farms Middle School in Collierville, Tennessee, celebrated with a "morp" dance—a parody of a traditional prom. The kids dressed in T-shirts and jeans for the shindig, which also featured wacky moves from several faculty members. Students earlier had voted with pennies to decide which teachers would compete in a dance contest. A history instructor took the top prize by incorporating calisthenics into his routine. "When you have students that are that motivated, we have to support them," the school's librarian told the *Commercial Appeal* (Hanna, 2004).

NO. 10

The Pour House

Raise a glass for students at a wine tasting.

Funding Sources: Ticket sales, concession sales, product sales, sponsorships

Potential Haul: > $5,000

Possible Partners/Sponsors: Wine shops, restaurants, corporate donors

SUCCESS SNAPSHOTS

- How big can a school's wine-tasting fundraiser be? Well, the annual Wine, Stein, and Dine function that benefits Idaho's Post Falls School District recently featured the fruits of more than 85 wineries in addition to a big selection of micro-brews and dishes whipped up by local restaurants, the *Spokesman-Review* reported (McNeish, 2006). Culinary adventurers pay $40 in advance and $50 at the door for three hours of food and drink, a silent auction and a raffle, and fun extras like a recent attempt to set a few world records. In its first decade, the event helped the district's education foundation pour forth more than $160,000 in grants. Meanwhile, New Jersey's Marlboro Educational Foundation recently teamed with a wine shop and a local fine dining restaurant to put on a wine-tasting event coupled with a four-course meal—generating $7,000 for the Marlboro district ("Wine-Tasting," 2006).

   It's no wonder more PTOs and school foundations have turned to wine tastings as a faster-paced replacement for the traditional banquet. As the *Chicago Daily Herald* noted, where banquets might provide a "too passive" experience, "the popular wine tastings draw big crowds, who mingle from station to station while they sip wine and purchase wine—in large quantities" (Daday, 2006). Wine is sold at discounts that still enable merchants (who often help fundraisers with these events in the same way that bookstores pitch in to put on school book fairs) to funnel some cash back to education.

- You might just develop a crush on this next idea: California's Malibu Family Wines holds an Annual Harvest & Crush Event that raises money for arts education ("Malibu Family Wines," 2006). The highlight is the "barefoot grape crush" that lets visitors try their hands—or feet, in this case—at an old winemaking technique. They can then receive a botanical foot soak from representatives of a local salon before moving on to the tasting (which features no foot-stomped wines). Guests also can participate in a silent auction while sampling savories provided by area restaurants.

- Jazz bands seem to go well with wine tastings, but the Rotary Club's annual fundraiser for California's Redlands

Unified School District was dubbed Red Wine & Blues because it serves up blues music along with the vino, the *San Bernardino County Sun* reported (A. Bennett, 2006). "It's not one of those snooty wine tastings," one organizer said. "It's really fun. It's more of a Saturday night party." Now in its third decade, the event relies on a local wine shop to coordinate the participation of some 50 wineries, which tempt the taste buds of about 500 guests.

🅢 Windows & Wine: A Very Tasteful Fundraiser was on tap in Buchanan, Michigan, recently, the *South Bend Tribune* reported (Frasieur, 2006). An auction of painted windows, as well as old chairs from Ottawa Elementary, followed the tasting. The organizers planned to offer a nifty tie-in line of artistically painted wine bottles at future fundraisers.

ADDED ATTRACTIONS

🅢 Because there's a bit of a fear factor for many folks when it comes to sampling and selecting wines, it's smart to market tastings as fun, no-pressure, educational experiences. Consider posting some tasting tips online in advance of the event, for instance, or inviting a laid-back local expert to ease people through the experience. "There's so much snobbery attached to wine these days and people are sometimes a little bit scared" (Murray, 2006), Paul Burrell told the *Poughkeepsie Journal* recently before attending a charity tasting. Burrell knows snooty: he served as Princess Diana's butler for a decade and helped put on parties for royalty and heads of state. He offers the following tips for wine tastings fit for a king (or queen):

   o "Make sure your Chardonnay is well chilled."
   o Pour shiraz at room temperature a few minutes after decanting the bottle. "Let it breathe for a while."
   o Serve sparkling wines and Champagnes in celebration glasses. "Tall, elegant flutes will retain its sparkle and vitality."
   o Pair the wines with "nibbles, not a banquet. You shouldn't serve messy foods. Make them small and compact so you can easily handle them."

- Here's a bonus food-pairing tip, from master sommelier Andrea Robinson (Miltner, 2005): that well-chilled Chardonnay goes great with popcorn! Robinson (formerly Andrea Immer) has produced several down-to-earth books and DVDs on wine tasting. For more information, visit www.andreaimmer.com.
- When serving alcohol, hold the event off school grounds, resolve any liquor license issues well in advance, restrict attendance to adults 21 and older, make sure bartenders understand they should not overserve patrons, and have designated drivers on hand to ferry home anyone who becomes impaired.

NO. 11

Daring to Sing

Tune in to a karaoke challenge.

Funding Sources: Donations, concession sales

Potential Haul: < $1,000

Possible Partners/Sponsors: Nightclubs, civic groups

SUCCESS SNAPSHOT

- Invite local organizations to put together teams for a karaoke night with a twist. Encourage participants to pay $5 or $10 for the opportunity to dare anyone in attendance to sing a specific song. The target can then choose either to perform the tune or pay double to pass along the dare to someone else—perhaps even the person who put them on the spot in the first place. This fundraiser is most likely to enjoy success if it includes groups of people who know each other well—coworkers, fellow club members, parents, teachers, and the like. But it can work even better if it features groups that enjoy a friendly rivalry with each other, such as pitting the police department against the fire department or faculty members and families against their counterparts at competing schools. If possible, enlist a local nightspot to host the festivities. Alcohol consumption (in moderation, of course) tends to help amateur singers get into the spirit of the evening. And if you bring in a big crowd on an off night, you might even score a cut of the bar's take.

NO. 12

Treasure Hunting

Send donors off on a wild scavenger hunt.

Funding Sources: Entry fees

Potential Haul: > $5,000

Possible Partners/Sponsors: Corporate donors

SUCCESS SNAPSHOT

⑤ Taking advantage of the ease and immediacy of digital photography, two West Chicago, Illinois, organizations that provide afterschool programs to needy children recently held a Digital/Polaroid Camera Treasure Hunt, the *Chicago Daily Herald* reported (Randle, 2005). The entry fee was $25 per car and included a map of the town, clues to finding local landmark "treasures," pizza for all participants, and raffle prizes for winning teams who showed up with photographic proof they'd found all the sites—either with digital or Polaroid shots. In addition to being a fun variation on the traditional scavenger hunt, it's an inexpensive event to put on.

ADDED ATTRACTION

⑤ Taking a cue from reality TV, the San Carlos, California, district's annual Amazing Race has turned into a fun way to increase parental involvement and raise money for schools, the *San Francisco Chronicle* reported (Murphy, 2004). The 2004 event netted nearly $10,000 from six parent teams who bid for the privilege of competing in a wacky scavenger hunt race filled with puzzles and physical challenges all across San Francisco. Winning teams earned lottery tickets and commemorative caps. But most racers also went home after a sunset dinner cruise with the urge to sign up for future races. Challenges included retrieving clues from the bottom of swimming pools, swallowing pickled mackerel, forming a bucket brigade, and riding tricycles around a city block. "I was kind of overwhelmed by the amount of planning and the complexity that went into it," said one parent. "At the end of it, we all said, 'Next year, we're going to do it again.'"

CHAPTER SIX

Starring Students

NO. 13
Spellbinding Solicitations

Host a student spell-a-thon or "celebrity" spelling bee featuring administrators, teachers, and other prominent smarty-pants locals.

Funding Sources: Pledges, ticket sales, concession sales, sponsorships

Potential Haul: > $5,000

Possible Partners/Sponsors: Bookstores, corporate donors

SUCCESS SNAPSHOTS

- ⑤ After 300 K–5 students correctly reeled off the spelling of 7,274 words, Wright Elementary in Des Moines, Iowa, earned $2,500 in pledges to support school assemblies focused on character education, the *Des Moines Register* reported (Kane, 2006). For their efforts, participants were rewarded with extra recess and a beach-themed party. In preparation for the event, the children studied word lists and took a practice exam. Meanwhile, the school sent a letter and pledge sheet to parents and asked them to help solicit pledges for every word their kids got right during the spell-a-thon.

⑤ The University of Alaska–Anchorage brings in upwards of $20,000 annually from its BizBee event in which local businesses pay for the privilege of fielding teams for a spelling competition, the *Anchorage Daily News* reported (Cox, 2003). Wacky rules rule the day—and help generate extra cash and excitement. For instance, teams can pay to spring a difficult word on an opposing crew, and the group selling the most tickets for a related raffle gets a free pass it can use to avoid having to spell one word. In addition, the team that shows up with the biggest cheerleading squad earns a free shot at exchanging one of its words with an opposing crew. Spicing up this recipe for fun are volunteers in bumblebee suits who tap the heads of losing contestants with wands. All the money goes toward adult literacy education.

⑤ A student spell-a-thon at Newport Elementary in Newport Beach, California, raked in $17,000, which helped the school avoid laying off instructional aides, the *Newport Beach Light* reported (Rhoades, 1999). All children who aced a precontest spelling exam were invited to enter; 130 qualified and got three weeks to study up and gather pledges. Contestants were divided into three sections: first and second grade, third and fourth grade, and fifth and sixth grade. Nearly 200 parents, teachers, and other interested adults watched the competition unfold.

ADDED ATTRACTIONS

⑤ Kick off the event with a choral performance of "Why We Like Spelling," "The Spelling Rules," or other songs from the Tony-winning Broadway musical *The 25th Annual Putnam County Spelling Bee*. Find out more at www.spellingbeethe musical.com.

⑤ Keep the theme going with a special screening of the inspirational 2006 film *Akeelah and the Bee* (rated PG), which Pulitzer Prize–winning critic Roger Ebert called "particularly valuable for young audiences" (Ebert, 2006). Or try the

2002 documentary *Spellbound* (rated G), which follows eight National Spelling Bee contestants on their wild word quests.

NO. 14
Paging Profits

Uncover nifty ways to jazz up your book fair.

Funding Sources: Book sales, sponsorships

Potential Haul: $1,000–$5,000

Possible Partners/Sponsors: Bookstores, publishers, speaker's bureaus, authors

SUCCESS SNAPSHOTS

- To bolster its library budget, Orion Elementary in Redwood City, California, has been holding an annual Children's Book Author & Illustration Faire since 2003, the *San Jose Mercury News* reported (Krieger, 2006). One recent event featured eight writers and artists who volunteered to attend. They "were treated with the kind of reverence usually saved for rock icons and heads of state," the paper noted. "Students brought them chairs and cups of water, then asked for autographs and advice." An associated book sale is run by a local store, which donates 20 percent of the proceeds to Orion. At the last fair, that meant about $2,500 for the school library—more than double its annual $1,000 book budget. An enterprising parent started the fair by drafting a list of 450 contemporary children's authors and illustrators and then calling her way down the list. How eager are such creators to connect with young readers? In the first year, the parent extended six invitations—all of which were accepted.
- Spurring donations with a uniquely personal touch, Terrace Elementary in Ankeny, Iowa, brought in $500 for

new library books during the first half of a recent school year, the *Des Moines Register* reported (Pieper, 2006). In its first two years, the school's "birthday book" program added more than 100 titles to the shelves while giving students a sense of excitement, pride, and ownership. Each fall, the school asks parents to support the library with a small donation. Students whose families give are then invited to look at fresh shipments as they arrive and designate one text as their birthday book. The child's name and donation year are inscribed on a bookplate, which adorns the first page. Each kid gets the first crack at checking out his or her book. "They just think it's fun," the school's media specialist said of the honored students. And even when the children inevitably move on, their books will remain to delight and inform future generations.

🄢 Chocachatti Elementary in Brooksville, Florida, put extra zing into a recent book fair with a Camp Read-a-Thon event, the *St. Petersburg Times* reported (Wasserman, 2006b). Pajamas-clad students entered a cafeteria that had been transformed into a forested campsite, complete with orange paper flames blowing in a fire ring. After snuggling into their sleeping bags, the children listened as a succession of guests read favorite stories. Teachers and parent volunteers painted campers' faces and served up s'mores, while older children dressed as bears to greet and entertain the younger kids. Proceeds from the book fair enabled the school to provide every student with free yearbooks.

Proving that great organizations sometimes think alike, the PTO for Walnut Street Elementary in Dover Township, New Jersey, hit on a similar theme for its recent Spring Scholastic Book Fair, the *Asbury Park Press* reported (Delaney, 2006). Organizers set up Camp Read-a-Book in the school gym. They borrowed tents and camp chairs from a local scout troop and set up a fire consisting of logs and cellophane flames. Kids ate marshmallows off of sticks while listening to stories read aloud by special guests. Peer counselors from a nearby high school served refreshments, while teachers and parents kept things running dressed as camp counselors, complete with hiking boots and neckerchiefs. "It's a great event to promote reading and a good way to stock up on books for summer reading," one organizer noted.

⑤ School book fairs don't have to be held at school these days. Increasingly, organizers are hooking up with local independent or chain bookstores to host day- or week-long events during which students, parents, and other school supporters submit special vouchers when making purchases. Typically, 20 percent of the proceeds from such sales go back to the school group. That's what happened recently in South Tampa, Florida, where Mabry Elementary held its book fair at a nearby Barnes & Noble outlet because the school's media center was under construction, the *Tampa Tribune* reported (Poltilove, 2006). In addition to distributing vouchers to the school community and suggesting books parents might buy and donate to the new media center in honor of students or favorite teachers, organizers staged several readings for children during the week-long event, along with scavenger hunts and even origami workshops. At such book fairs, customers also can request vouchers right at the store or print them out from school Web sites.

⑤ Tennessee's Farmington Elementary recently combined its Scholastic Book Fair with a community open house that included a barbecue dinner, the *Commercial Appeal* reported (Keenan, 2006). But the event, with a "kingdom of reading" theme, kicked off earlier in the day when students arrived to discover that the front of the building and the lobby had been decorated like a medieval castle. Teachers even dressed up as royalty and knights. Kids who showed up in costume were entered into a free book drawing. At the evening book fair, titles were grouped by areas of interest and reading levels. In addition to buying books for their children to take home, parents also purchased texts for school use from classroom wish lists drawn up by teachers.

NO. 15

Model Behavior

Put on a stylish school fashion show.

Funding Sources: Ticket sales, clothing sales, sponsorships, concession sales

Potential Haul: $1,000–$5,000

Possible Partners/Sponsors: Clothing stores, salons, modeling studios

SUCCESS SNAPSHOTS

⑧ In a variation on the classic fashion show fundraiser, in which students model clothing borrowed from local shops for paying audiences, juniors at Rogers High in Newport, Massachusetts, sauntered down the runway in new and vintage dresses and formal wear that businesses had actually donated for sale, the *Providence Journal* reported (Peoples, 2006). Dozens of outfits were sold at the event for $5–$40. The class netted more than $1,000 to cover prom expenses while outfitting many of its members for the dance at bargain prices.

⑧ Attendees of the annual LiLu Fashion Show at California's Mira Loma High gave a hand to handmade handbags, the *Sacramento Bee* reported (Wiener, 2006). The LiLu Handbag Project was started in 2000 by teens named Libby and Lucia, who came up with the title by combining the first two letters of their names. Every year, students sew up a storm of classy purses and kicky clutches for the show, which charges admission of $5 for students and $10 for adults. The bags are auctioned at the end of the event for an average of about $50 each, with proceeds going to support a center for homeless teens. One teen organizer passed on a great tip for all student runway walkers: "Try to go slow. What happens is, everyone rushes through their walks so they can get off the catwalk as soon as possible."

⑨ Fancy hats from around the world were on parade during the Celebrate Our Heritage fashion fundraiser for the Ethnic Heritage Museum in Rockford, Illinois. The event also sold hatbox centerpieces decorated by local artisans, hosted hat-making activities for children, and invited attendees to wear their favorite hats, the *Rockford Register Star* reported (Westphal, 2006a). A similar school event might make a good centerpiece for a cultural diversity celebration. Bonus tip: Other organizations have hosted successful fundraisers focused on hairstyles.

⑨ Taking its cue from popular reality TV series *Project Runway,* a Detroit cancer charity initiative gave 50 local fashion designers two weeks to come up with beautiful ball gowns that cost no more than $100 to produce, the *Detroit News* reported (Morrison, 2006). The winner of the competition, which was judged by a *Project Runway* contestant, took home a donated prize package worth about $5,000—and the benefit sold out its 250 tickets the day after 10 finalists were selected. A somewhat smaller-scale event focused on student designers likely would make a great school fundraiser.

⑨ Underscoring the fact that many potential variations exist for fashion fundraisers, the owner of a Corona, California, yoga studio enlisted students to show off their moves during a runway show, which also featured classical Indian and belly dancing. The yoga and dance performances took place while models walked the runway and guests dined on sushi and wine. The hip happening brought in $10,000 for children's vaccinations and other needs, the *Inland Valley Daily Bulletin* reported (Shadia, 2006). "It's a fresh approach to fundraising," said one participant. "It's always good to learn something new and incorporate fun with health and fitness." Think about what special artistic resources you might tap in your community to supplement a school fashion event.

⑨ Getting all dolled up is the order of the day at the American Girl fashion shows, which nonprofit organizations around the nation use to raise funds. During the shows, girls dress up to match favorite American Girl dolls. The events have raised millions of dollars for charity since 1992, the *Rockford Register Star* reported (Westphal, 2006b). Heavy on mother-daughter fun, the fashion festivals feed off the popularity of the American Girl line, which has sold some 111 million books and 12 million 18-inch dolls since the company launched in 1986. Our Lady of the Lake School in Mandeville, Louisiana, recently combined its first American Girl fashion fundraiser with a fancy tea party, the *Times-Picayune* reported (Shriner, 2006). "The program provides an entertaining and educational look at how generations of American girls have used clothing to express their own unique style and personality," a school administrator noted. For information on setting up an American Girl fundraiser, visit www.americangirl.com, click on "About American Girl," and then select "Corporate Philanthropy."

Ⓢ Seven Atlanta schools participated in a *purr*-fect fashion fundraiser, with more than 500 students covering T-shirts in animal-inspired art, the *Atlanta Journal-Constitution* reported (Scholten, 2006). The sartorial masterpieces were hung at a local mall where shoppers were invited to donate a dollar and vote for their favorites. After about two weeks of voting, the top 25 finishers modeled their artistic shirts as part of the Paws for Style Fashion Show and Parade. A related silent auction featured T-shirts decorated by prominent members of the community. The event was the centerpiece of the mall's effort to raise $10,000 for local schools and animal shelters.

ADDED ATTRACTIONS

Ⓢ Create oddball appeal by turning your event into an animal fashion show. You can even solicit donations from pet-loving locals for the privilege of walking their decked-out dogs and cats down the runway. (For additional ways to incorporate furry friends into fundraisers, turn to item No. 32, Pet Smart.)

Ⓢ How about a time-warp fashion show focusing on styles from the 1920s, 1970s, or 1980s? You could feature vintage threads or new pieces inspired by the theme era.

- Ⓢ Some folks avoid fundraisers because they think they'll drag on too long. Here's one way to change their minds: bill your event as a 60-minute or 30-minute fashion show—and stick to the schedule. One student dance troupe from Norco, California, even put on a 10-minute fashion show as part of a fundraiser, the *Press Enterprise* reported (Lou, 2005). But that event also included an hour-long dance performance.
- Ⓢ Amp up the fashion show by enlisting local club DJs or up-and-coming bands to play while the models strut their stuff. Many acts will be happy for the exposure—and glad to pitch in for a good cause. If they have ties to the school, all the better.

NO. 16

Record-Setting Haul

Enlist students to set a world record.

Funding Sources: Pledges, ticket sales, sponsorships

Potential Haul: > $5,000

Possible Partners/Sponsors: Civic groups, corporate donors

SUCCESS SNAPSHOTS

- Ⓢ More than 305,000 Florida middle school students capped off the first month of the 2006–07 academic year by setting the world record for most people simultaneously reading aloud, the *Miami Herald* reported (Gibson, 2006). The event, which promoted a statewide reading initiative called Shoot for the Stars, featured an excerpt from the *Peter Pan* update *Peter and the Starcatchers* by Dave Barry and Ridley Pearson. To make the reading officially eligible for inclusion in the *Guinness Book of Records,* organizers enlisted 1 adult witness for every 20 kids.

⑨ Duke University beat the University of North Carolina 3,688 to 3,444 in the world's longest basketball game, the *Herald-Sun* reported (Ferris, 2006). The 12-player teams battled under the baskets for 57 hours, 17 minutes, and 14 agonizing seconds. The shot clock remained in effect throughout as referees watched the action in shifts and players napped at courtside when they weren't among the 10 active competitors. The athletes were not allowed to leave the gym for more than five minutes at a stretch, but they were permitted six fouls every two hours. Nearly 400 volunteers supported the teams with everything from food and medical treatment to live entertainment. The January 2006 game, which raised $60,000 for North Carolina's Hoop Dreams Academy, finished to a packed house and earned live national TV coverage.

⑨ Captain Spaulding and Rufus T. Firefly would have felt right at home at Ringgold High in Ringgold, Georgia, on January 12, 2006. That's when 1,571 students, teachers, and staff members convened at the school stadium to set the world record for most people wearing Groucho Marx glasses at the same time and place, the *Chattanooga Times Free Press* reported (Cooke, 2006). The event raised bushy eyebrows for 15 minutes—as well as money for the American Cancer Society. Said one senior of the plastic specs, "They hurt my face, but it's fun."

⑨ Stadium High in Tacoma, Washington, marked its 100th anniversary in 2006 by hosting an event billed as the world's largest school reunion, the *News Tribune* reported (Abe, 2006). In a quest to beat the previous official record of 2,521 attendees, alumni of more than 10 classes held reunions at Stadium High simultaneously. Now that's a record worth shooting for. Not only are the numbers achievable, but bringing thousands of alumni back to campus at the same time would be a fantastic fundraising opportunity.

ADDED ATTRACTIONS

⑨ Carefully follow the rules for recording your record-setting attempt. Guinness officials have disallowed many otherwise successful attempts due to a lack of proper documentation. For complete guidelines, go to www.guinnessworldrecords.com.

- Ⓢ Hold your event on Guinness World Records Day, which comes around every November. Check the Guinness Web site listed above for details. You can attempt to set a mass-participation record or direct students (and others) to simultaneously try for an individual mark.
- Ⓢ Consider setting a record no one has ever attempted before. Between November 2005 and November 2006, Guinness World Records officials approved 2,244 brand-new records.
- Ⓢ Try for a record that ties into a core learning goal—like the Minnesota school that promoted reading by attempting to craft the world's largest pop-up book, as the *Star Tribune* reported (Kumar, 2002). Here are some other possibilities to get your creative juices flowing (*Guinness*, 2006). The Guinness record for Most People to Write a Story is 757, set in 2006 at a children's literature festival in Verona, Italy. New York City's Ashrita Furman set the Pogo Stick Jumping–Distance mark in 1997 by hopping 23.11 miles in 12 hours and 27 minutes. Falmouth, Maine's Parkfest Sandcastle Committee erected the World's Tallest Skyscraper, which topped 29.25 feet, in 2003. And 637 fur- and fun-loving folks gathered in London in 2005 to form the Largest Gathering of People Dressed as Gorillas. That last event was a fundraiser for the Dian Fossey Gorilla Fund.

NO. 17

Freeform Fundraising

Maximize student participation with a "do-your-own-thing-a-thon."

Funding Sources: Pledges

Potential Haul: > $5,000

Possible Partners/Sponsors: Corporate donors

SUCCESS SNAPSHOT

⑨ Read-a-thons, jog-a-thons, skate-a-thons, bike-a-thons, and even bowl-a-thons are all popular pledge-based fundraisers. But St. Luke's Lutheran school in Itasca, Illinois, generated excitement among students by replacing its walk-a-thon with a Do-Your-Own-Thing-a-Thon, the *Chicago Daily Herald* reported (Wilson, 2004). Organizers hoped to top the walk-a-thon's record haul of $25,000 in pledges and matching donations. While younger kids jumped in bouncy castles, skipped rope, in-line skated, or even rode scooters, many of the older students participated in marathon volleyball tournaments. "I'm excited that there isn't just one thing to do," said one 8-year-old. "I'm going to ride my red scooter."

ADDED ATTRACTION

⑨ Rio Norte Junior High in Valencia, California, successfully rebranded its combination walk-a-thon/jog-a-thon as a "fitness challenge," the *Daily News of Los Angeles* reported (Rock, 2005). The event generates more than $30,000 annually for the school's physical education department. In one recent year, some 1,200 students and 250 parents and Rio Norte employees trekked a total of 5,000 miles around the half-mile track over two days. "Kids this age don't have enough big events," one phys ed teacher said. "They're so used to seeing extreme this and extreme that, we have to keep up with that."

CHAPTER SEVEN

Sporting Chances

NO. 18
Tee Time

Drive up receipts with a variation on the classic golf tournament.

Funding Sources: Ticket sales, concession sales, sponsorships

Potential Haul: > $5,000

Possible Partners/Sponsors: Golf courses, corporate donors

SUCCESS SNAPSHOTS

⑤ The dead of winter doesn't stop golfers in Wausau, Wisconsin, from playing in an annual charity tournament. But with local courses closed for the season, they take their clubs (as well as baseball bats, brooms, paddles, and even leaf blowers) to frozen Lake Wausau for the Ice Tee Classic, the *Wausau Daily Herald* reported (Berkhahn, 2006). Business and social groups sponsor and create the course's 11 holes—good exposure to the 150-plus participants who pay $20 (or $50 per family) to play. Instead of honoring the winners—it's tough to call it a fair game when the leaf-blower guy keeps getting holes in one—organizers award door prizes randomly, along with a trophy to the player wearing the most creative costume.

§ Even with glow-in-the dark balls, players toted flashlights to stay on course at the Nite Light Golf Tournament in Wellington, Florida, the *Sun-Sentinel* reported (Shakes & De Los Reyes, 2006). The event, which raised money for educational scholarships, included wine-tasting stations along the abbreviated course.

§ The Hawaii Soccer Association's over-50 squad stuck their cleats into the game of golf and twisted until they came up with a "soccer golf" fundraiser, the *Honolulu Advertiser* reported (Wai, 2002). About 70 participants kicked and putted soccer balls through large, croquet-style wickets that stood in for golf holes. "It was the most fun fundraiser we've ever done," said one organizer. "Everyone seemed to like it; it didn't matter how old they were. It was new and it was a challenge, and skill level didn't matter. We tried to make some of the holes easy and some holes challenging." The game proved so popular that the club had to set up extra rounds. "People got really competitive when they compared their scores with someone that they knew," the organizer noted. "They wanted to go again and better their scores."

§ What better way to raise money for little kids than through miniature golf? Kindergartners at Wilson Primary Center in South Bend, Indiana, recently designed mini-golf holes and then invited families to play the course (constructed with parental help) for a dollar a round, the *South Bend Tribune* reported (Gallagher, 2006). Some 200 people picked up the sticks during the two-hour festivities. Meanwhile, students at O.E. Dunckel Middle School in Farmington Hills, Michigan, put their math and science lessons to use in crafting a mini-golf course with a "planets of our solar system" theme. The set-up was later used for a $2-per-round fundraiser. "It is pretty interesting to make angles to make sure you get a hole-in-one, and learn about the planets we're doing," one student told the *Detroit Free Press* (Powers, 2006).

ADDED ATTRACTIONS

- ⑤ For a fun fling, try a disc golf tournament. It's based on regular golf, but instead of swinging clubs at a ball, players throw Frisbee-style discs weighted for different distances. The goal: Toss the disc into a metal basket in as few throws as possible. But unlike their traditional counterparts, disc golfers regularly finish rounds in less than two hours, and they seldom lose their discs. Many communities sport 9- or 18-hole disc golf courses in local parks—as well as affiliated clubs whose members raise thousands of dollars a year for good causes.
- ⑤ Combine one of the tournament styles above with a hole-in-one contest—or the golf-themed fundraising idea in No. 19 next.

NO. 19

Drop the Balls

When numbered golf balls fall from the sky, schools win.

Funding Sources: Raffle sales

Potential Haul: > $5,000

Possible Partners/Sponsors: Golf courses, corporate donors

SUCCESS SNAPSHOTS

- ⑤ A fundraiser in Ankeny, Iowa, invited donors to buy numbered raffle tickets with a prize of either $1,000 or a big-screen television, the *Des Moines Register* reported (Danley-Greiner, 2006). Instead of drawing the winners from a hopper, however, each ticket corresponded to a numbered golf ball. A fire truck ladder lifted a container holding the balls next to a golf course fairway, then dumped the load. The ball that landed nearest the hole held the winning number.

- ⑤ A Cuyahoga Falls, Ohio, fundraiser upped the ante by dumping more than a thousand numbered golf balls onto a practice green from a helicopter, the *Akron Beacon Journal* reported (Cardwell, 2006b). Participants chipped in 10 bucks a ball for a shot at cash prizes.

ADDED ATTRACTIONS

- ⑤ Combine a ball drop with a rubber duck race for a one-two, land-sea punch. Eden, North Carolina, calls its event the Rubber Duck Regatta. Myrtle Beach, South Carolina, calls its contest the Great American Duck Race. Baldwinsville, New York, hosts the Great River Duck Race. Adamstown, Pennsylvania, gets in the swim with the FireQuacker 1000. And Moncks Corner, South Carolina, puts on the Million Dollar Duck Race. No matter the name, these races tend to have several things in common. People are invited to "adopt" numbered rubber duckies, usually for $5 each. The ducks are then dumped into a river en masse, where they bob downstream into a catch net. Commonly, the first five or so ducks that float over the finish line earn prizes for people holding tickets with corresponding numbers. The biggest duck races have raised more than $100,000 for sponsor organizations. (Be sure to check applicable laws on raffles and lotteries before proceeding.)

  The Million Dollar Duck Race adds an extra wrinkle: if a duck corresponding to a certain number drawn before the race in lottery fashion crosses the finish line first, the lucky ducky holding the matching ticket takes home a cool million bills, the *Post and Courier* reported (Graham, 2005). With nearly 6,000 ducks taking a dunk, the odds of the right one winning the race are low, but the possibility undoubtedly gooses sales. By the way, that race sells its ducks for $5 but also offers a $25 "six-quack."

- ⑤ Organizations interested in holding a high-dollar-prize duck race, hole-in-one contest, or half-court basketball shot competition can obtain a prize indemnification insurance policy that will handle the payout in the unlikely event someone hits the big score, the *Memphis Business Journal* reported (Harris, 2006). Most insurance agents don't write such policies directly but will usually steer interested clients to specialty insurers, such as Nevada-based Hole in One International. Insuring a hole-in-one contest with a million-dollar prize might cost around $2,000, for instance, depending on the length of the hole and number of contestants. The policies require winning-shot eyewitnesses for payouts— and the big moment may have to be caught on video to secure extremely large prizes.

⑤ Entice corporate sponsorship by auctioning off the opportunity to have all of the golf balls and/or ducks embossed with the winning bidder's logo.

NO. 20

Hoop Dreaming

Score with a three-on-three basketball tournament.

Funding Sources: Entry fees, ticket sales, concession sales, sponsorships

Potential Haul: > $5,000

Possible Partners/Sponsors: Professional and semipro basketball teams, athletic centers, corporate donors, civic groups

SUCCESS SNAPSHOTS

⑤ Students played hoops for the troops recently at Lakewood Middle School in Overland Park, Kansas, the *Kansas City Star*

reported (Kan, 2006). The three-on-three basketball tourney drew more than 30 teams willing to pay the $15
entrance fee and be guided to greatness by teacher sponsors.
The squads squared off in six-minute preliminary matches
that weeded the field down for semifinal and championship
rounds. More than $500 in cash and $200 in calling cards
came in to help the son of an instructor serving in Iraq.

⑤ Richmond, Indiana, recently crowned three royal hoop-
sters with its first Kings of the Court 3-on-3 Classic benefiting a local community center, the *Palladium-Item*
reported (Bennett, 2006). The half-court tourney
included high school and adult divisions, as well as
dunking and three-point-shot contests. The top three
teams in each division took home trophies; the entry fee
was $25 per player.

⑤ A two-day Street Basketball Festival proved a big score for
the Salvation Army Boys and Girls Club of Horry County,
South Carolina, the *Myrtle Beach Sun-News* reported
(Wilson, 2006). The three-on-three basketball tournament
included 10 age brackets and a wheelchair division. Team
entry fees ranged from $100 to $250, depending on
bracket. Each squad was guaranteed to play two games,
and the event also featured a slam-dunk competition with
style points awarded by local celebrity judges. Said one
organizer, "We wanted a festival that transcended basketball and concentrated on the celebration of teamwork, fair
play, and athleticism."

ADDED ATTRACTION

⑤ Three-on-three basketball is a half-court game. Teams can
have a fourth player for substitution purposes. Most games
are played to 15 points, with baskets counting for 1 point
each—or 2 points for shots made from beyond what's usually
the 3-point stripe. For more rules, check out the University
of Chicago guidelines at http://athletics.uchicago.edu/
campus/3on3/rules.htm.

NO. 21

Mascot Madness

Have a field day with the district's costumed characters.

Funding Sources: Ticket sales

Potential Haul: < $1,000

Possible Partners/Sponsors: Corporate donors

SUCCESS SNAPSHOTS

- Judging by the popularity of events such as the annual Mascot Hall of Fame induction competition, folks enjoy seeing school mascots at work and play. The online hall was recently written up by columnists at the *Detroit News* (Rubin, 2006) and other papers, who exhorted readers to vote for local favorites. Imagine bringing together all of the school mascots in your area for an afternoon of fun, games, and fundraising.

- Bruno the Brown Bear recently bested the Penn Quaker in a wrestling bout to become Ivy League Mascot Champion, the *Brown Daily Herald* reported (Hewson, 2006). The match apparently was a sideshow event at Wrestlemania 22 in Rosemont, Illinois. The costumed clowns outdid the antics of the most outlandish professional wrestlers by taking after each other with brass knuckles and taking the bout into the bleachers. The mayhem continued for several minutes—and several falls—thanks to the "fact" that the referee lay unconscious in the ring during most of the match.

- Every January, the Universal Cheerleading Association, Dance Team, and Mascot National Championships take place in Orlando, Florida, the *Orlando Sentinel* noted (Shrieves, 2003). College mascots submit two-minute performance videos in the fall, and a panel of judges selects 10 to compete at the Disney World Resort. The lucky young men and women lug their costumes to a final competition that gives them each three minutes to wow an audience of cheerleaders, parents, and other fans. Perhaps there's an all-district school mascot variety show and competition in your fundraising future.

CHAPTER EIGHT

Artistic Attractions

NO. 22

Appraising Treasures

Throw an *Antiques Roadshow*-style event at which people can pay to have cherished heirlooms appraised.

Funding Sources: Ticket sales, sponsorships, concession sales

Potential Haul: > $5,000

Possible Partners/Sponsors: Auction companies, estate appraisers, antiques shops, corporate donors

SUCCESS SNAPSHOT

⑨ For its Trash or Treasure fundraiser, the St. Louis Science Center actually landed the stars of the PBS hit *Antiques Roadshow*. They were on hand to appraise the items folks brought in from their attics, basements, and garages in hopes of hearing they were sitting on an antique gold mine, the *St. Louis Post-Dispatch* reported (Oyola, 2006). It's unlikely that Leigh and Leslie Keno will pitch in at a similar event to

71

raise money for your school, but you can hold an appraisal fundraiser just the same by asking local collectibles experts, antique shop owners, and estate sales professionals to lend a hand. While you're at it, ask the librarian to dig up the latest major collectibles prices guides for on-site reference.

NO. 23

Picture This

Target discerning donors with a student art show and sale.

Funding Sources: Ticket sales, art sales

Potential Haul: $1,000–$5,000

Possible Partners/Sponsors: Art galleries, art supply shops, museums, civic groups, malls

SUCCESS SNAPSHOT

⑤ Every year since 2002, four Sacramento, California, schools have participated in the High School Self-Portrait Show at the 20th Street Gallery, the *Sacramento Bee* reported (Ranganathan, 2006). About 80 students display and sell their artworks after being juried into the show. Gallery staffers help them price the pieces, but they don't take a cut of the proceeds. The artists take home 80 percent of the sale price, and the remainder is donated to charity. The show also brings in a professional artist to judge a portrait competition featuring cash prizes. "The whole notion of the starving artist is usually someone without any business sense," said the director of the arts program at a participating school. "We want them to learn to present themselves in a professional manner. These kids are now realizing there is a market, and if they pursue it and concentrate on it, they can make a name for themselves."

NO. 24

Chair-itable Artworks

Auction off furniture painted by students and other local artists.

Funding Sources: Ticket sales, art sales, concession sales

Potential Haul: > $5,000

Possible Partners/Sponsors: Art galleries, art supply shops, furniture stores, civic groups, malls

SUCCESS SNAPSHOTS

- Ⓢ Chair-adise was the colorful name given a chair-painting fundraiser for Ohio's Mariemont School District, the *Cincinnati Enquirer* reported (Howard, 2005). The event auctioned 16 chairs—including everything from thrones and rockers to bar stools and park benches—decorated by Cincinnati-area artists to support programs such as continuing teacher education and textbook acquisition.

- Ⓢ The 15 adult-size chairs and 4 doll versions auctioned at a fundraiser for Key School in Annapolis, Maryland, featured art inspired by children's storybooks, *The Capital* reported (Winters, 2005). Attendees didn't have to submit winning bids to share in the magic, however, as the school was smart enough to sell commemorative posters featuring the chairs for $20, along with note card packages for $12. Organizers promoted the event by displaying the chairs at a local mall bookstore, where kids decked out in storybook-themed attire paraded one Saturday afternoon while their fathers read stories aloud to passersby. The whimsical creations included a Tarzan chair complete with its own palm tree as well as seats based on *Where the Wild Things Are, The Secret Garden, The Catcher in the Rye,* and *A Wrinkle in Time.* Also of note was a chair inspired by the Shel Silverstein story *The Giving Tree*; it was decoupaged with thousands of textured paper scraps and then coated with varnish.

⑨ Artists gussied up 32 Adirondack rocking chairs for a YMCA fundraiser in Oswego, New York, called Chair-ish the Y, the *Post-Standard* reported (O'Toole, 2006). Before auctioning off the chairs, the organization displayed them at area businesses, which each paid $150 for the privilege.

⑨ Painted chairs and other wooden furniture were sold at a silent auction for hurricane victims put on by the students of Renaissance School in Appleton, Wisconsin. The Chairs for Charity—Artists Helping Artists event also sold homemade desserts and treated attendees to dance and theatrical performances. "I wanted it to be more than just a silent auction of the furniture so that all of our artists would be able to help out with the event, as well as draw as many people as possible from the community," the teen organizer told the *Post-Crescent* (Berthiaume, 2006).

⑨ In a distinctive twist on the concept, an Albuquerque, New Mexico, nonprofit group invited high school clubs and other local student groups to participate in a Youth Chairity Rock fundraiser. Each registered group was given one rocking chair to decorate for later auction, the *Albuquerque Journal* reported (Lovato, 2006). The teens then used the chairs as the centerpiece of dance performances at the event. Prominent local artists also chipped in chairs for the sale.

ADDED ATTRACTIONS

⑨ Here's a great variation on the theme for band fundraisers: Orange Park Junior High in Jacksonville, Florida, capped off one of its spring band concerts with a silent auction of artistically reimagined music stands that had been headed for the trash heap. More than a dozen members of a local art guild pitched in on the project, the *Florida Times-Union* reported (Maraghy, 2006). How'd they look? "Awesome," the guild's president said. "They seem to float in the air, if you can imagine that."

⑨ Speaking of artistic reclamation projects, why not paint worn-out classroom desks for sale as garden planter holders instead of throwing them away or sending them into storage when the school gets replacement furniture?

NO. 25

Feeling Scrappy

Make memories—and money—with a school scrapbooking night.

Funding Sources: Ticket sales, supply sales, concession sales, sponsorships

Potential Haul: $1,000–$5,000

Possible Partners/Sponsors: Scrapbooking shops, art supply shops

SUCCESS SNAPSHOTS

⑨ Scrapbooking is a wholesome family hobby that's grown into a huge phenomenon in recent years. Practitioners combine journaling and commemorating special events with cherished photos and arty filigrees that can turn plain pages into accomplished, highly personal works of art. Many scrapbookers enjoy working side by side with other hobbyists in a modern update on the old-fashioned quilting bee. They also enjoy sharing new photo-cropping and decorating techniques. All of those factors combine to make scrapbooking a wonderful tie-in for a school fundraiser.

At Brooksville Elementary in Brooksville, Florida, for instance, families recently gathered for a Valentine's Day Scrapbook Night, the *St. Petersburg Times* reported (Wasserman, 2006a). Earlier in the week, students completed essays describing what they loved most about their families. Those assignments then became the centerpieces of scrapbooks, which also included photos brought in by parents and supplies provided by the local PTA. "With the holiday and all the preparations for testing, this will be a nice, stress-free break from that," a PTA official noted. "It's a relaxing, bonding experience for parents and children."

⑨ A scrapbooking fundraiser in Clemmons, North Carolina, enlisted seven area crafts stores to donate materials for goodie bags, the *Winston-Salem Journal* reported (Barksdale, 2003). Participants attended seminars on new techniques taught by shop owners and other skilled scrapbookers, then gathered to try out the tricks on their own creations. Organizers guaranteed spots at the craft tables—as well as lunch—to advance ticket purchasers to spur early sales.

⑨ Crop for Our Kids proved to be such a successful fundraiser for Michigan's Livonia Public Schools in 2005 that the district turned it into an annual scrapbooking event, the *Detroit News* reported (Esparza, 2005). The inaugural outing drew some 90 hobbyists and brought in $3,000. With local businesses donating food and raffle prizes, the proceeds went directly to instructional support programs. The owner of a local scrapbooking shop, who set up a supply table at the event, ticked off several reasons why it's easy to build fundraisers around the hobby. First, it's an inexpensive pastime with multigenerational appeal, and it doesn't require a big venue. Also, "You can make a lot of money in a one-day event," she said. "It does not take much."

NO. 26

Playing Around

Delight young and old by auctioning off fancy playhouses.

Funding Sources: Ticket sales, auction proceeds, concession sales, sponsorships

Potential Haul: > $5,000

Possible Partners/Sponsors: Developers, architectural firms, building contractors, art galleries, corporate donors, malls, home improvement stores

SUCCESS SNAPSHOT

⑤ How can you turn a school auction into one of the hottest family tickets in town? Try offering an array of cool custom playhouses for sale. That's what one California non-profit has been doing every year since 1992 with its Project Playhouse auction, the *Orange County Register* reported (Medina, 2005). HomeAid Orange County fills a large tent in a mall parking lot with guests, even though it charges a steep $40 for adult tickets and $15 for kids ages 4–12. (Family four-packs run $90, a $20 discount.) Including corporate sponsorships, the event now brings in more than $400,000 a year. Its appeal lies in a parade of about a dozen dream playhouses that generate as many oohs and aahs as auction bids. The fundraiser also includes a party with refreshments.

The group raffles off one playhouse every year to give everyone a shot at bringing home a custom model. The rest are auctioned, with bids starting at $5,000. Recent creations have included a replica White House, complete with a miniature Oval Office, and a small-scale baseball stadium. Sale prices typically range from $15,000–$25,000. Local homebuilders construct and donate the lavishly appointed, 8-by-10-foot houses, which remain on display at the mall for more than a month. (During weekend open houses, visitors can pay $5 to peek into the homes; but at the main event, they can actually explore inside them.) Another great aspect of the event: "This charity involves kids," one organizer noted. "I get to see the smiles on their faces as they run through the playhouses." For more information, visit www.projectplayhouse.org.

NO. 27

Throwing a Disc

Record and sell instant CDs of musical performances.

Funding Sources: Product sales

Potential Haul: < $1,000

Possible Partners/Sponsors: Music stores, electronics retailers

SUCCESS SNAPSHOT

- ⑨ Parents and others who attend student concerts at Douglas Anderson School of the Arts in Jacksonville, Florida, can buy freshly recorded CDs of each performance as they're walking out the door, the *Florida Times-Union* reported (Kormanik, 2005). Students in the school's media sound classes serve as recording engineers and have discs packaged and ready for sale no later than eight minutes after the audience applauds for the last time. After one jazz night, the CDs brought in $600, with each disc selling for $6 (four-packs were offered for $15—great for sending to far-flung relatives). "It's kind of hectic, but it's really fun," said a student who helped package the CDs hot out of the recorder. The school also holds a spring CD release party to sell discs featuring selections from winners of its annual songwriting contest.

ADDED ATTRACTION

- ⑨ This is a cool fundraiser, but the technical requirements might seem a bit daunting. In addition to experimenting with microphone placement, for instance, it's important to assemble an equipment package that will deliver decent live recording quality and quick CD-burning capabilities. When it comes to audio recording, the next innovation always lies just around the corner, but there are a few Web sites worth checking out to learn more about recording and duplicating performance CDs. For instance, the Florida Bandmasters Association has endorsed several hardware packages. For details, visit www.flmusiced.org/fba/technology/cd _recorder_deals.htm.

Also, the DePauw University Band has been recording CDs of its performances since 1996. It employs the services of New York-based Mark Custom Recording Services, Inc., which sells packages of live recording equipment. To learn more, visit www.markcustom.com. Although such packages often cost $1,000 or more, your school's A/V department might have some or all of the equipment on hand to do a decent job.

NO. 28

Band on the Run

Set up musical performances where people will least expect them.

Funding Sources: Donations

Potential Haul: < $1,000

Possible Partners/Sponsors: Music stores, malls

SUCCESS SNAPSHOT

- As part of a Charity Week during which 26 student clubs raised nearly $20,000 in five days—not a bad idea in itself—Illinois's Lake Zurich High sent marching band members to supermarket parking lots. There, they played impromptu gigs in the back of a pick-up truck, the *Chicago*

Daily Herald reported (Scalf, 2003). The distinctive holiday music performances left smiles on shoppers' faces and earned a few hundred dollars in donations.

ADDED ATTRACTION

⑤ Where else could marching band members set up to delight potential donors? And what about sending string quartets, choirs, and even small theater troupes out on the town for similar fundraising performances? Showcasing a school's artistic programs in fresh, unexpected ways can help enrich the cultural life of the community while generating needed cash.

CHAPTER NINE

Animal Antics

Flamingo Flocking

Plant plastic pink flamingoes in the yards of unsuspecting victims—for a price.

Funding Sources: Donations

Potential Haul: $1,000–$5,000

Possible Partners/Sponsors: Garden supply stores

SUCCESS SNAPSHOT

- Some school groups really do wing their fundraisers—by sending flocks of pink plastic flamingoes to homes all over town. Here's how it works. After securing anywhere from 12 to 120 of the wire-legged birds, organizers charge $20, $50, or more to "flock" someone's yard. (Some groups use flocks of a set size, while others charge by the bird). Donors select their targets for reasons ranging from playing a prank on a friend to marking special occasions such as birthdays, graduations, and anniversaries. The flamingoes usually show up while homeowners sleep. The victims wake up to find the flock and a letter describing the fundraiser and ways to pass along the fun. Some groups promise to remove the birds after 24 hours, while others leave them on display for up to a week if the victim doesn't pay to send them somewhere else. (People who don't wish to play along can have the lawn ornaments picked up immediately at no charge, but that happens rarely.) Smart frills include offering antiflocking "insurance" for people who want to contribute but don't want to deal with the birds and charging an extra fee to tell victims who sent the flamingoes their way.

In addition to leaving an explanatory flier along with the birds (on pink paper, if possible), smart organizers plant a sign explaining the prank to passersby—complete with a phone number for ordering a flocking—to drum up more business. It's also best to publicize a flamingo "season" of a month or so to keep the novelty from wearing off. Ambitious groups have been able to earn upwards of $5,000 with this infectious novelty act before it flies south for the winter. It's not hard to figure out why. As one teen event organizer in Johnson County, Kansas, described it to the *Kansas City Star,* "We would see the person come out and their face just lit up with laughter. I think everyone just loved it" (Sederstrom, 2005).

ADDED ATTRACTION

⑤ It's usually not easy to pinpoint the origin of a fundraising idea, but the *Times Union* in Albany, New York, tracked down the people who say they started the flamingo-flocking tradition in 1991 (Lopez, 2005). Twins Rick and Ralph Fazio claim they hit on plastic pink flamingoes as hot fundraisers after planting several on a cousin's lawn as a joke. In 1992, they pitched the Flamingo Surprise at an Ohio home-and-garden show as a great way to celebrate birthdays and anniversaries. By the end of the year, Ralph Fazio said, the brothers were fulfilling 300 orders a month. "Then people started copying us all over the country," he added. Find out more at www.flamingosurprise.com.

NO. 30
Living the Wild Life

Enchant the community by displaying whimsical animal sculptures all over town.

Funding Sources: Sponsorships, auction proceeds, raffle sales

Potential Haul: > $5,000

Possible Partners/Sponsors: Art galleries, art supply companies, civic groups, corporate donors

SUCCESS SNAPSHOTS

⑨ Take advantage of the community-art fundraising craze Chicago created in 1999 with its Cows on Parade installation—320 fiberglass cows painted by artists and arrayed around the central city's sidewalks that generated $3.5 million for local charities while drawing a million gawking, pointing tourists. All it takes is a set of thematic fiberglass sculptures (usually animals), artists to give them unique looks, public display space, a wacky slogan, and a fun auction finale. Enlisting local businesses to sponsor the pieces generates additional cash. Coeur d'Alene, Idaho's 2004 No Moose Left Behind installation brought in more than $350,000 for a local education foundation, the *Spokesman-Review* reported (Crane, 2005). The next year, nearby Spokane, Washington, set loose 40 customized Kodiak bear sculptures for Bear Necessities, a Friends of Ronald McDonald House fundraiser. In 2006, the same organization loosed beautifully painted carousel animals on the city's streets. Said the artist who created the Kodiak bear, "When I was working on the model of the full-size sculpture, the first child to see it went right up to it and hugged it. I knew then we were onto something."

⑨ Residents of (and visitors to) Great Falls, Montana, recently embarked on The Buffalo Hunt to find 26 bison bulls and 4 calves displayed around the small city. The project, which took nearly two years to execute, was staged as a playful answer to a community art event called The Horse of Course across the state in Billings, the *Great Falls Tribune* reported (Wilmot, 2005). A local sculptor created the buffalo model used by Minnesota-based FiberStock, Inc. to fabricate fiberglass versions. Participating artists received small materials stipends to make their mark on the animals but donated their time. (Area high school students decorated the four calves and kept them on campus for permanent display.) Organizers approached businesses to sponsor the bulls for $3,000, $5,000, or $10,000 each. The minimum pledge covered the purchase price of one sculpture. Sponsorships brought in $105,000 as well as $95,000 of in-kind contributions.

Before allowing the bison to stampede onto the sidewalks of Great Falls, event leaders protected them by building sturdy bases and giving the animals two blasts of clear coat at a local auto dealer's body shop. After a summer on display, the animals were sold off at a gala auction. "I've done a lot of fundraising, and I know this to be true: If your cause has integrity, if you believe in it and translate that to the community, you achieve your goal," the event chairwoman said (Wilmot, 2005).

⑨ These fundraisers usually feature animal sculptures—but there's no law that says they have to. More than 80 gussied-up fiberglass guitars hit the streets of Phoenix during a GuitarMania event that raised money for a chapter of Big Brothers and Big Sisters, the *Arizona Republic* reported (Sowers, 2005). Teen artisans at Phoenix Country Day School took on one of the 10-foot guitars as a project, adorning it with recycled materials and dubbing it "Renew, Reuse, Recycle." Theirs was one of 62 commercially sponsored sculptures, which were displayed along with 21 guitars decorated by Arizona-based celebrities, including singer Stevie Nicks and guitar legend Eddie Van Halen. The first GuitarMania installation, held in Cleveland in 2002, raised $1 million for nonprofit groups.

ADDED ATTRACTION

- ⑤ In addition to fabricating fiberglass bison for the Great Falls, Montana, project profiled here, Minnesota's FiberStock, Inc. has crafted similar sculptures for community-art fund-raisers across the nation. For more information, visit www .fiberstock.com.

NO. 31

Circus Maximus

Invite the big top to town to perform for your school.

Funding Sources: Ticket sales, concession sales, sponsorships

Potential Haul: > $5,000

Possible Partners/Sponsors: Civic groups, corporate donors, malls

SUCCESS SNAPSHOTS

- ⑤ The big top meant big bucks recently for the District 59 Education Foundation in Elk Grove Village, Illinois, the *Chicago Daily Herald* reported (Ter Maat, 2006). The organization contracted with the Oklahoma-based Kelly Miller Circus and earned $10,000 from four performances of the one-ring extravaganza over two days. The circus is on the road about 250 days each year and often performs for school fundraisers. Kelly Miller pitched its tent near Elk Grove High and played to appreciative audiences, who paid $8 to $25 per seat. Three years earlier, the circus performed a two-show fundraiser in nearby Lincolnwood, Illinois, for the Lincolnwood School District 74 Parent Teacher

Association. The 90-minute performances included elephants, clowns, trapeze artists, and other traditional circus trappings. Ticket prices for those shows started at $10. "We were looking for a family-centered event," a PTA official said. "We wanted something that the entire community could enjoy" ("PTA Fund-Raiser," 2003).

Ⓢ An international youth circus jumped through hoops to raise money for Consolidated School in Kennebunkport, Maine, the *Portland Press Herald* reported (Sayer, 2006). Circus Smirkus arrived with 30 teen performers who put on four shows in two days, wowing kids of all ages with acrobatic, aerial, juggling, and clowning feats (the last ones no doubt decked out in snazzy clown shoes). The performers stay with host families wherever they set up their ring. "They are pretty amazing kids," a PTA official said. "The fun of it is that it's kids doing the show for elementary school kids. It's pretty spectacular—kind of like a Cirque du Soleil for children." After securing donated space for the performances, the school received a cut of ticket and concession sales from the nonprofit circus, which also travels with its own band. All told, Vermont-based Circus Smirkus has brought in more than $2 million for fundraisers since it launched in 1987.

Ⓢ Passaic County, New Jersey's Garfield High raised money for its Class of 2007 graduation party with three days of performances by the Cole Bros. Circus of the Stars, the *Herald News* reported (Kays, 2006). After playing to more than 5,000 fans under its red-and-yellow big top, the circus handed over about $6,200 to the school. "I do a lot of fundraising and it's usually beefsteak dinners and raffles— not the circus," one parent organizer said. "But it's a good time and it's a good cause."

Ⓢ Every year, the auditorium at South Carolina's Cottageville Elementary transforms into a one-ring circus for a PTO fundraiser, the *Post and Courier* reported (Paras, 2006). For $2 to $3 a ticket, kids and parents crowd in to see Florida's Wonderland Circus present acts ranging from prancing poodles to fire-throwing jugglers and high-flying trapeze artists. The small troupe also features a rope-trick specialist and a trick bicycle rider. "It's a Cottageville tradition," the principal said. "As hard as it is to raise funds, this makes it real easy."

❺ Florida State University's Flying High Circus showed up at the football field of Seminole High in Seminole, Florida, recently to raise cash for nearby Bauder Elementary, the *St. Petersburg Times* reported (Estrada, 2006). The college performers juggled, flew high on the trapeze, walked the high wire, and completed acrobatic tricks for more than 1,000 local residents. "The circus will come back to Bauder," promised the president of the school's booster club. "It was one of our best fundraisers yet."

ADDED ATTRACTION

❺ If you're ready to run away with the circus—or at least book one for a school fundraiser—here's a select list of troupes that play such engagements. One note of caution: Several of these circuses employ animal acts, which can prove controversial in some communities. It's important to check the troupe's animal-handling track record before booking performances. And now, on with the shows:

  o **The Amazing Anastasini**. This Florida-based troupe is run by the Anastasini family, eighth-generation circus performers. In addition to its Big Top Spectacular, the group also sends smaller acts onto the road and adapts its shows to indoor and outdoor venues. Visit www.anastasini.com.

  o **Big Apple Circus.** Founded in 1974, the New York-based group's Circus to Go program promises custom-tailored acts for fundraisers large and small: "Strolling performers mix and mingle with guests, spotlighted specialty acts add a splash of wonder to any occasion, skilled teaching demonstrations enhance educational and team building workshops, and circus-themed stage shows are the perfect solution to your 'featured entertainment' needs. Our creative staff will work with your theme and space to design the perfect performance fit." Visit www.bigapplecircus.org.

  o **Carson & Barnes Circus**. Founded in 1937, this Oklahoma-based troupe brings its big top to more than

200 cities and towns every year. Qualifying organizations can book the circus with a $495 up-front payment and a $2,500 guarantee. Visit www.circusfundraiser.com.

o **Circus of the Kids.** This Florida-based organization offers fundraising performances, one-day school assemblies, and in-school residencies that impart circus skills to students. Visit www.circusofthekids.com.

o **Circus Smirkus.** Founded in 1987, this Vermont-based troupe offers extended school residencies that teach students circus skills they then demonstrate in an assembly. The circus also performs at fundraising events. Visit www.circussmirkus.org.

o **Cole Bros. Circus of the Stars.** Billed as the "World's Largest Circus Under the Big Top," this Florida-based, three-ring outfit performs in 115 cities annually and is available for fundraisers. Its crimson-and-gold tent can accommodate nearly 3,000 patrons. Visit www.colebroscircus.com.

o **Flying High Circus**. This Florida State University student troupe regularly performs fundraising shows, at lengths ranging from 30 minutes to 2 hours. The circus can bring its own big top or adapt its performances to various indoor and outdoor venues. Acts include juggling, trapeze, teeterboard, and many others. Visit www.circus.fsu.edu.

o **Kelly Miller Circus**. Founded in 1938, this Oklahoma-based group performs two 90-minute shows on its 1-day fundraising stops. Its big top seats 1,500. It is a sister organization to the Cole Bros. Circus. Visit www.kmcircus.com.

NO. 32

Pet Smart

Host a dog- and cat-friendly celebration.

Funding Sources: Ticket sales, concession sales, sponsorships

Potential Haul: > $5,000

Possible Partners/Sponsors: Animal rescue organizations, pet supply stores, civic groups, corporate donors

SUCCESS SNAPSHOTS

- An annual Bark & Whine Ball entertains canines and their human companions in San Francisco to raise money for injured cats and dogs, the *San Francisco Chronicle* reported (Bigelow, 2006). In addition to serving up human buffet fare, the event includes a silent auction of pet accessories along with live music for anyone wishing to walk the dog on the dance floor. Tickets range from $75–$2,500 plus $20 per pooch. But only one human is allowed per dog—or maybe it's the other way around!
- A Friends for Life Pet Photo Contest allows Montgomery, Alabama, animal lovers to pony up $10 for a chance of getting their favorite pet photo published in the local humane society's next calendar, the *Montgomery Advertiser* reported (Greene, 2006). Submitted snaps go on display in a local mall food court, where diners can pick their favorites for $1 per vote.
- At Frankfort, Kentucky's annual Critterpalooza, visitors and their leashed canine companions are treated to a pet parade, live music, silent auction, sweet treats, and dog obedience demonstrations—all for $10 (children under 16 get in free), the *Lexington Herald Leader* reported (Hudspeth, 2006).

  Similarly, Greenville, South Carolina, throws a Bark in the Park fundraiser every year that features displays of dog agility (don't call them stupid pet tricks), a demonstration of police K9 techniques, a blessing of the pets, and a Walk of the Dogs walk-a-thon with prizes for pooches who bring in the most scratch, the *Greenville News* reported (Nichols, 2006). Other award categories include "happiest expression" and "waggiest rear end." The donations and $5 pet entry fee help raise up to $30,000 annually. "It's an opportunity for dog owners to bring their pets to a function that actually is geared towards the animals," one organizer said.

Another Bark in the Park—this one in Belleville, Illinois—entertains big crowds with a dog-owner look-alike competition, canine costume contest, and Pooch Smooch, the *St. Louis Post-Dispatch* reported (Meehan, 2006). "Those smooches go on and on," one organizer said. "The owners and their dogs are exceptionally close. They aren't afraid to smooch in public." Sounds like PDDAs—public displays of *doggie* affection. Tickets cost $25 ($15 for children under 16). All three events benefit animal-support groups.

ADDED ATTRACTIONS

- Ⓢ If your community doesn't already support a big annual pet-themed fundraiser, this would be a perfect opportunity to team up with an animal-assistance group and split the proceeds.
- Ⓢ Many of these events have a pet health component as well, hosting low-cost vaccination clinics and even pet-massage specialists.

NO. 33

Hitting the Spot

Play cow, horse, or chicken bingo to enjoy the smell of money.

Funding Sources: Raffle sales, concession sales

Potential Haul: > $5,000

Possible Partners/Sponsors: Farms, ranches, dairies, corporate donors, 4H Clubs

SUCCESS SNAPSHOTS

⑤ Here's the poop on a somewhat vulgar fundraiser appropriate for *manure* audiences only. The Greater New Orleans Therapeutic Riding Center enlisted its horses to participate in a "plop drop" on a field marked off with 400 squares, the *Times-Picayune* reported (Thompson, 2005). Guests purchased $10 tickets that could return $2,000 if a horse dropped a road apple on the corresponding spot. Two heats meant two big winners, and the silly fun also included smaller-scale chicken plop drops and a cow pie–flinging contest. Proceeds supported riding lessons for children with disabilities.

⑤ Cow Patty Bingo was the name of the game at Olive Branch High in Olive Branch, Mississippi, when 300 people showed up at the school's baseball field to see one lucky ticket holder walk off with $10,000, the *Commercial Appeal* reported (Oliver, 2005). Tickets for the 3,000-plus, three-by-three-foot squares went for $10 each. The cow walked the fenced-in field for an hour and a half before nature finally called and a big winner was declared. The school's total haul topped $20,000 after the prize money was paid out.

⑤ Organizers of Cow Chip Bingo in Barrington, Rhode Island, had their event down to a science, the *Providence Journal-Bulletin* reported (Pina, 2001). The cow had a designated feeding time of 45 minutes before the game began. Once the animal was released onto the Barrington High football field, the scoreboard clock was set to 30 minutes—all the time allotted for her to make a patty. And for it to count, it would have to measure at least three inches in diameter and three inches high. When the cow failed to deliver, a drawing of the $10 tickets was held to award the $1,410 top prize—as well as second- and third-place windfalls of $500 and $250. About 600 $10 tickets were sold, leaving the local Pop Warner Football program flush with funds.

⑤ After raising three cows from birth, Future Farmers of America members at Don Lugo High in Chino, California, loaned out their animals for a Cow Chip Bingo fundraiser benefiting nearby Brea Canyon High and Brea Olinda High, the *Orange County Register* reported (Nicholson, 2000). Each of the first three plops earned a lucky ticket holder a cash prize of

$1,000, $500, or $250. After selling just over 1,000 of the 2,000 available squares, the schools netted about $3,200.

⑤ If you can round up some elephants, you might be able to copy a fundraiser held by South Africa's Bryanston Primary School. Its Dumbo Drop Day awarded around US$4,000 to the biggest winner (Business Wire, press release, February 16, 1998). Organizers created an 8,600-square field on which three elephants were released for six hours. Holders of corresponding tickets were guaranteed prizes if one of the elephants dropped dung on their squares. A drawing of winning tickets was held at the end of the day to award the grand prize. Representatives of an accounting firm certified the results. While the elephants and their handlers wandered the fenced field, attendees were treated to a craft fair, live music, magic shows, clown performances, pony rides, and refreshments.

⑤ New band uniforms were the goal of the Pony Plop put on recently by Florida's Umatilla High School Band Aids ("Nighttime-Naturalist Program," 2006). When the pony pooped, one ticket holder claimed a $1,000 prize. A thousand tickets were sold for $10 a pop, and the event also featured a silent auction and fish fry. Meanwhile, at California's Valencia High, the football team put on a Donkey Derby in which three donkeys were loosed on the field while holders of 3,000 $5 tickets looked on, the *Daily News of Los Angeles* reported (Darvish, 2005). But instead of spending hours chalking 3,000 squares, team coaches used a computer model of the field to create a virtual grid with corresponding measurements for determining which tickets earned the $1,000 top prize and two $500 consolation awards for the second and third plops. And finally, the organizer of several cow-chip bingo fundraisers in Colorado and California offered a tip for making sure the event doesn't drag on for hours: feed the animal alfalfa hay soaked in molasses. "There can't be too many places in the world where people get excited when a cow goes," he told the *Denver Post* (Obmascik, 1997). "As a fundraiser, this works. It really works."

CHAPTER TEN

Service Smiles

NO. 34

Recycling Revenues

Bag profits by providing specialty recycling services to the community.

Funding Sources: Recycling proceeds, service fees

Potential Haul: > $5,000

Possible Partners/Sponsors: Recycling centers, corporate donors, environmental organizations, civic groups

SUCCESS SNAPSHOTS

⑤ "Wouldn't it be nice if, just once in a while, [schools would] come up with a fundraiser that wouldn't cost you money?" the Worcester, Massachusetts, *Telegram & Gazette* asked recently (Lilyestrom, 2005), as it reported on a great way to generate cash while performing a public service and helping to protect the environment. Students at Leicester Primary School signed up with the popular FundingFactory recycling program, which pays groups for sending in old cell phones and used printer ink cartridges. In the initiative's first year, the children solicited donations only from family and friends, earning a respectable $800 for their efforts. The next year, they expanded the project to the entire community and looked forward to raising thousands of dollars annually. The director of a local recycling center even allowed the students to pick up phones and cartridges dropped off there. FundingFactory also sends prepaid shipping containers to area businesses that wish to support a given school's recycling fundraisers. For more information, visit www.fundingfactory.com. The site also includes classroom lesson plans related to recycling.

⑤ Here's a fundraising idea worth phoning home about: Bryan Elementary in Coeur d'Alene, Idaho, recently rustled up funds to send fourth graders on a field trip to see the state legislature in session by collecting used cell phones from parents and other members of the community, the *Spokesman-Review* reported (Ball, 2005). Bryan is one of thousands of schools sending the defunct devices to a company called EcoPhones, which pays between $1 and $300 per cell phone, depending on model and condition. (Most of the donated phones net fundraisers a buck.) In addition to bringing in needed cash, the program keeps batteries out of waste facilities and teaches children about the importance of recycling electronics. For more details, visit www.ecophones.com.

⑤ The recycling club at Georgia's Dalton High raised $7,000 in 2005 alone after enlisting residents and 30 local businesses to chip in cell phones and printer cartridges, the *Chattanooga Times Free Press* reported (Braly, 2006). Said the environmental science teacher who founded the club, "I'm trying to get a good cross-section of the community involved so that, say, one accounting firm can tell another one about it, or one dentist can tell another dentist. I tell people, 'If it prints or you can talk on it, give it to us.' There's a value to garbage."

ADDED ATTRACTIONS

⑤ America Recycles Day, held every November, provides a strong fundraising tie-in. More than 20 high schools in

Broward County, Florida, teamed up to collect tens of thousands of pounds in recyclables, such as newspapers, phone books, and glass jars, on that day in 2005, the *Sun-Sentinel* reported (Thorpe, 2006). For tips on starting a similar fundraiser, visit www.americarecyclesday.org. Another good Web resource: www.earth911.org.

⑨ Earth Day, marked in the United States on April 22, gives schools another fine opportunity to conduct environmentally friendly fundraisers. For example, Clark Memorial Library in Carolina, Rhode Island, hosts an electronics recycling event every Earth Day, charging a modest fee to help residents get rid of unwanted televisions, computers, and monitors, the *Providence Journal* reported (Zuckerman, 2006). Landfills consider such items toxic waste because they leach lead, mercury, arsenic, beryllium, and cadmium into the ground—so recycling them is very important. For more information on Earth Day, visit www.earthday.gov.

NO. 35

Cleaning Up

Pitch in around town on yard work and chores for a fee.

Funding Sources: Service fees, sponsorships

Potential Haul: > $5,000

Possible Partners/Sponsors: Lawn care providers, contractors, home improvement stores, civic groups, corporate donors

SUCCESS SNAPSHOTS

⑨ Students at Bellingham, Washington's Explorations Academy joined adult volunteers recently to earn more than $2,500 doing yard and garden projects for local homeowners during a day-long event called Blisterama, the *Bellingham Herald* reported (Lei, 2006). Meanwhile, on a Saturday dubbed Rent-a-Wrestler Day, Hamilton Southeastern High in Fishers, Indiana, set loose its wrestling team to perform odd jobs and chores around town for $10 an hour, with a minimum booking of 2.5 hours ("Wrestlers Available," 2006).

⑤ More than 100 pupils at New Jersey's Monmouth Junction Elementary probably amazed their parents by going all out for a Kids Making Cents Chore-a-Thon, which raised money for a library expansion, the *Home News Tribune* reported (Ismail, 2004). The idea is simple: ask parents and other family members to chip in a certain amount whenever the student completes select chores during the fundraising period. Students committed to helping out around the house on everything from making lunches to taking out the garbage and folding laundry. Similar events undertaken by other area schools had previously raised $800 to aid victims of a pipeline explosion and $10,000 for 9/11 memorials in Plainsboro and West Windsor. Such fundraisers also may include a character-building component. "Children no longer are doing chores," asserted the coordinator of the Monmouth Junction event. "Parents have forgotten this sense of responsibility and they need to restore it."

⑤ When eighth graders at St. Anthony of Padua School in North Akron, Ohio, roamed the halls carrying books and performing other tasks for younger children, it was all for a good cause, the *Akron Beacon Journal* reported (Cardwell, 2006a). The students raffled off their services at 25 cents a ticket to raise $300 for a local man injured in a farming accident.

ADDED ATTRACTION

⑤ Why not ask parents with home improvement skills to volunteer for a Handyman Day on which they'll complete small projects for local homeowners and donate their fees to the school? They could even take their children along as tool-holding assistants. Boost the event's appeal by asking local contractors to donate a few hours of labor, too. Advertise in senior centers to reach a group of people likely to need a hand around the house (Joachim, 2003).

NO. 36
Baby Booming

Brand your school as the go-to spot for child care during citywide events.

Funding Sources: Service fees, sponsorships

Potential Haul: < $1,000

Possible Partners/Sponsors: Child care centers, toy stores, civic groups, corporate donors, colleges

SUCCESS SNAPSHOT

⑤ Jackson Elementary in Norman, Oklahoma, transforms into a temporary day care center whenever the University of Oklahoma football team plays at home. School parents volunteer to watch children dropped off by Sooners boosters up to an hour before game time, the *Oklahoman* reported (Anderson, 2003). The football fans then pick up their kids no later than an hour after the game ends. The PTA charges $25 per child for the much-appreciated service, generating hundreds of dollars every game. Interest ran so high that the organization was considering advertising in the hometown papers of visiting teams to alert their incoming fans of the option as well.

NO. 37

Classic Car Car Wash

Buff up the standard car wash by catering to sweet rides.

Funding Sources: Service fees, exhibitor fees

Potential Haul: < $1,000

Possible Partners/Sponsors: Car clubs, auto dealers, auto supply stores, civic groups, malls

SUCCESS SNAPSHOT

⑨ Transform a standard car wash fundraiser into something special by focusing on classic cars. Enlist members of a local car club to array their sweet rides around the designated parking lot to create a strong visual impact—and give passing motorists an extra incentive to pull in. Advertise special discounts—and promises of tender loving care—for washing autos that are at least 25 years old. Car buffs are always looking for an excuse to congregate, show off their vehicles, and salivate over other classics. So if you spread the word of this event well enough, you might just find yourself hosting an impromptu auto show. Just pick a sunny weekend day and start your fundraising engines.

ADDED ATTRACTION

⑨ Some groups skip the car wash and just host a car show fundraiser. That's what an Ohio Head Start Parent Group did recently, generating entry fees for 69 vehicles and creating a fun community event in the process, the *Coshocton Tribune* reported (Austin, 2006). A mobile DJ spun golden oldies while car and truck owners competed for prizes and

Wal-Mart shoppers enjoyed an eyeful of classic Detroit steel. "This is the best fundraiser we've ever had, so it might turn out to be a future event," one organizer said.

NO. 38

Send in the Dads

Enlist fathers and other men in the school community to team up for a memorable event.

Funding Sources: Ticket sales, concession sales

Potential Haul: > $5,000

Possible Partners/Sponsors: Civic groups, men's organizations, corporate donors

SUCCESS SNAPSHOTS

- Having fun with gender stereotypes pays off for a Florida community center that holds an annual Men Who Cook fundraiser. It features nearly a dozen local chefs cooking up gourmet grub for some 400 appreciative donors. Teens involved with the center act as servers on the big evening. "This is my favorite event," one restaurant owner told the *Bradenton Herald* (Wilcox, 2006). A similar fundraiser for the Lamar Consolidated Independent School District in Texas drew 56 manly cooks and more than 1,000 diners, who chowed down on dishes ranging from snapper Rockefeller to key lime pie, the *Houston Chronicle* reported (Rosen, 2003). The event brought in $52,000 for educational project grants.

- About 40 dads, granddads, teachers, and administrators put on a Fathers' Follies show that raised more than $2,000 for California's South Pasadena Middle School. "Men don't usually get involved in PTA-type events. The moms are usually the ones in the background organizing things," a female organizer told the *Pasadena Star-News* (Hoffman, 2006). "What makes this so great is that the dads are actually doing the work." Added a performer, "It's good for the kids, and it's good for the parents. You make friendships and establish relationships. Your girls are very embarrassed to see you out there, but I think they secretly love it."

❾ California's Community Preparatory School of Encanto revved up its annual Mother's Day fundraiser by hosting a lunch with an all-male fashion show called Visions of Men for dessert, the *San Diego Union-Tribune* reported (Peattie, 2006). More than 400 napkin-waving, picture-snapping moms enjoyed the festivities, which brought in about $9,500. Organizers sold roses the women could bestow upon their favorite models.

NO. 39
Celebrity Service

Enlist prominent locals and district employees to serve meals at a restaurant's school night.

Funding Sources: Donations

Potential Haul: $1,000–$5,000

Possible Partners/Sponsors: Restaurants, civic groups, corporate donors

SUCCESS SNAPSHOTS

❾ Michigan's Fowlerville Community Schools funds its DARE antidrug program in part through annual "celebrity server dinners" at the town's Olden Days Café, the *Detroit News* reported (Williams, 2006). In addition to enlisting teachers and administrators to wait tables, organizers ask other prominent local citizens to pitch in. The four-hour event, which includes live music and door prizes, brings in up to $1,200 a year. Meanwhile, the Mentor, Ohio, district partnered with a local eatery for its Celebrity Server Night featuring seven popular instructors and principals who pooled tips from appreciative students and their families, the *Plain Dealer* reported (Matzelle, 2004).

⑨ An Irvine, California, ice cream parlor hosted a sweet fundraiser for Northwood Elementary. Teachers spent an afternoon behind the counter, scooping up 12 percent of each sale for the school's PTA. Students and their families lined up at the Coldstone Creamery outlet to place orders with the team of instructors and engage in some afterschool banter, the *Orange County Register* reported (Lawrence, 2004). "We try to make it fun and we try to make it a social event for everybody," a PTA official said of the group's fundraisers. "The more connected you are to the school the more likely people are going to be to support the school."

⑨ Instructors and administrators at 20 schools in the Philadelphia area raised money for educational programs by waiting on students, parents, and other members of the community at McDonald's restaurants (Reveron, 2004). During one recent October, from 4:30 p.m. to 7:30 p.m. every evening when educators stepped behind the counters, a portion of the proceeds—plus tips—were earmarked for participating schools. "This is a great way to have fun while reinforcing McDonald's commitment to children and the community we serve," noted an official of the Greater Philadelphia Region McDonald's Operators' Association. Franchisees in many other regions feel the same way. In fact, the McTeacher's Night program has helped schools nationwide raise several million dollars, with each event generating an average $800 for the participating school (Chou, 2005). The initiative also helps schools forge community connections. As the principal of B.B. Comer Elementary in Sylacauga, Alabama, told the *Daily Home* after her school's 2006 McDonald's fundraiser generated $563, "Our teachers enjoyed the night. It was a fun opportunity for us to participate in the community and for students to see us out of our 'normal' surroundings. We told the students what we would be doing, but I think they were still surprised when they actually saw us there" (Jennings, 2006).

❸ The girls' volleyball team at Eastbrook High in Marion, Indiana, holds an annual table service fundraiser at a local pizza joint, which generates about $500 from tips and a cut of every buffet meal sold, the *Chronicle-Tribune* reported (Dicken, 2006). The longtime coach started the event in 2005 and has been pleased with the results. "It's an easy fundraiser," she said. "You show up. You get a dollar per buffet. You get to keep all the tips. You don't have to take orders or collect money. In three hours, we are done. Nobody is knocking on doors. Everybody has to eat somewhere, so it's not like buying a candle. It isn't somebody you know coming to you and you have to buy a candle from them."

NO. 40

Giving Directions

Hire out teens and adults to flag shoppers into stores.

Funding Sources: Service fees

Potential Haul: $1,000–$5,000

Possible Partners/Sponsors: Corporate donors

SUCCESS SNAPSHOT

❸ Drive down the commercial streets of most cities and suburbs on weekend afternoons, and you'll see people waving sales signs, often dressed in character, to entice shoppers into mattress shops, cell phone stores, pizza parlors, and the like. One teen soccer team in Richardson, Texas, took advantage of that phenomenon by creating a "human directionals" fundraiser in which members hired themselves out as living advertisements who waved customers into local businesses, the *Dallas Morning News* reported (Hughes, 2004). In one year, the initiative brought in nearly $3,000—and it proved much easier to pull off than the door-to-door product sales the team had tried in the past.

CHAPTER ELEVEN

Seasonal Successes

NO. 41

Scare Up a Maze

Find money by losing visitors in a haunted Halloween maze.

Funding Sources: Ticket sales, concession sales, sponsorships

Potential Haul: > $5,000

Possible Partners/Sponsors: Costume shops, theater groups, corporate donors

SUCCESS SNAPSHOTS

⑤ Some 30 volunteers amped up the fear factor at a haunted corn maze with a "jungle safari" theme in Danville, Indiana, the *Indianapolis Star* reported (Tuohy, 2006). The amateur actors, decked out as inhuman creatures, crafted creepy stories to tell any child who asked what had happened to them. They also swapped tips on being as scary as possible. Terrifying props are always effective, for instance, but the element of surprise produces the most shrieks.

"I'll sneak up on people before they even enter the maze," boasted one zealous zombie. "If I can scare a parent to the point that they trample their children running away, I know I've done my job." Incongruously, the $5 and $6 entrance fees went to a program that procures Christmas presents for needy kids.

❺ Transyl-Maze-ia was a Halloween highlight in Marion, Wisconsin, the *Post-Crescent* reported (Sherry, 2003). Teachers and students from several schools volunteered to portray the creepy cast at a local family fun park. Each school took charge of its own night, sending 30 warm bodies in exchange for a $250 donation from the park's operator. He painted a chilling picture of the fog-shrouded maze, which took about half an hour to work through:

> First you go through a simulated cornfield complete with cornstalks and hundreds of Christmas trees. Then you go through a barn with hayforks and a body. The woods are filled with werewolves. A fur trader's cabin contains pelts and a real live, freshly butchered buffalo head on the wall. Then you go through the mansion, dungeon, a tool shed, and the front porch of a farm house. A swamp and the cemetery is our finale, which I think is just incredible.

Sounds like a set-up worth emulating!

❺ Special education students at Mansfield High in Mansfield, Texas, raised about $1,500 by charging a buck a visit to their Scary Times Halloween maze, the *Fort Worth Star Telegram* reported (Ayala, 2004). Frights were foisted on revelers at every turn. As they progressed through the maze, they took a scary trip from the age of dinosaurs to the present day—with stops along the time line for Egyptian mummies, Dracula, and a King Arthur who enjoyed jumping out of the shadows.

❺ A Rotary Club fundraiser in Moorpark, California, brought in $20,000 for a Boys and Girls Club by setting up the Monster Maze at Tierra Rejada Farms, the *Ventura County Star* reported (Silkin, 1999). Rotarians constructed the labyrinth out of 300 garage doors its first year and, after scaring the socks off thousands who paid $6 each for the privilege, expanded to 400 the next. After making their way through a series of spooky set-ups, visitors were treated to a hayride down a deserted road and through a haunted barn.

ADDED ATTRACTION

- ⑤ Consider hosting a tamer version of the haunted maze in the afternoon for littler children so that everyone can get in on the creepy good times.

NO. 42

Seasonal Singing

Get into the holiday spirit by booking groups of carolers all over town.

Funding Sources: Service fees, donations

Potential Haul: $1,000–$5,000

Possible Partners/Sponsors: Civic groups, corporate donors

SUCCESS SNAPSHOT

- ⑤ Singing for Someone's Supper was a spirited December fundraiser put on by the Key Club at Montana's Choteau High, the *Great Falls Tribune* reported (Ogden, 2004). Students charged $30 to perform Christmas carols at local residences, businesses, hospitals, and nursing homes. Many of the sessions—especially those at the care facilities—were purchased as holiday gifts. All proceeds went to humanitarian causes.

NO. 43

Gingerbread Housing

Tempt holiday revelers with a parade of deliciously decorated homes.

Funding Sources: Entry fees, ticket sales, auction proceeds, sponsorships

Potential Haul: > $5,000

Possible Partners/Sponsors: Restaurants, cooking supply stores, candy shops, malls, civic groups, corporate donors

SUCCESS SNAPSHOTS

- Every December, the Children's Center for the Visually Impaired enlists Kansas City, Missouri's top pastry chefs to craft visually stunning gingerbread houses for an auction fundraiser, the *Kansas City Star* reported (Spivak, 2005). Typically, more than a dozen of the artistic houses go on display in the shops of the Crestwood neighborhood for several days before the Gingerbread Lane event. The evening kicks off with a panel of celebrity judges awarding prizes to several of the houses, which are then auctioned off. Attendees can preempt the bidding and take home a given house for $600. "It's such a relaxing, fun way to start off the holidays," one organizer said. "Everyone just shops and eats and helps a good cause."
- A Wichita, Kansas, fundraiser sets up a full Gingerbread Village at a local church, which visitors can explore for $5, the *Wichita Eagle* reported (O'Toole, 2005). Professional pastry chefs craft some of the houses, while others are created by families who take part in the two-day event. The houses are sold at a $75-a-plate dinner auction.

NO. 44

Polar Plunge

Heat up donations by dunking local notables in cold water.

Funding Sources: Pledges, sponsorships

Potential Haul: $1,000–$5,000

Possible Partners/Sponsors: Civic groups, corporate donors, media outlets

SUCCESS SNAPSHOT

⑤ Six principals joined several other school representatives and notable residents of Lafayette, Indiana, for a January Polar Bear Plunge into a local park pond under the watchful eyes of emergency rescue workers, the *Journal and Courier* reported (Richwine, 2004). The event ensured media coverage by enlisting radio and TV personalities to participate— always a smart idea for big school fundraisers. Besides injecting a bracing blast of levity into the dead of winter by sending the costumed do-gooders into the cold depths, the plunge brought in thousands of dollars for the Public Schools Foundation of Tippecanoe County. The cash went to Seeds for Excellence teacher grants, and prizes were awarded for "best costume" and "most pledges."

CHAPTER TWELVE

Cash Collecting

NO. 45

A Home Run

Raffle off a dream house to make your fundraising dreams come true.

Funding Sources: Raffle sales

Potential Haul: > $5,000

Possible Partners/Sponsors: Developers, real estate brokers, individual donors, home improvement stores

SUCCESS SNAPSHOTS

⑤ The North Idaho College Foundation launched its Really Big Raffle in 1994 as a way to raise money while giving carpentry students a challenging annual project—building a spec house from scratch. Every year, the college sells 5,000 raffle tickets at $100 each through participating local businesses. There are a few smaller prizes, but most eyes remain focused on the latest handsome house, which is open regularly for tours during the sales period. In July, ticket purchasers gather on a field at the Coeur d'Alene campus for a live drawing. The excitement is palpable (I know because I bought a ticket one year), and losing doesn't sting too badly when you realize that the cash will be used for scholarships, instructional grants, and other worthwhile activities.

§ Mater Dei High in Santa Ana, California, raffled off a million-dollar house in Costa Mesa for $200 a ticket. The school didn't cap the number of tickets sold but did throw in a second prize of a $10,000 shopping spree as a sweetener. "We thought it was a very creative and new idea to raise money," the school's president told the *Los Angeles Times* (Rivera, 2006).

§ Here's a smart marketing hook for one of these fundraisers: Mount Madonna School in California's Santa Cruz Mountains compared the odds of winning the beach house it raffled off with the chances of scoring the California Super Lotto jackpot, the *San Jose Mercury News* reported (Noguchi, 2006). The odds of hitting the lottery: 1 in 18 million. The odds of nabbing the house with a $150 ticket: 1 in 32,000. Plus, the school offered 319 smaller cash prizes, making the odds of winning something even better. The school also created a separate Web site for the fundraiser, complete with floor plan, photos, and map. As luck would have it, a childless local couple with a yen to support education sold the home to the school at below-market value under the condition that they remain anonymous.

ADDED ATTRACTIONS

§ Steve Martin used to perform a comedy routine in which he shared the secret for making a million dollars in real estate. "First," he said, "get a million dollars." Obviously, obtaining an expensive home isn't the easiest thing for most schools to do. But working with a local bank to put up a foreclosure property with a promise of a cut of the raffle proceeds might do the trick. Another possibility: Ask alumni to consider bequeathing a home to the school in their wills as a charitable donation; most won't, but one or two might. Don't dismiss an attractive fundraising idea as unrealistic until you apply some creative thought to the situation.

⑤ Don't go forward with a home-sale fundraiser until you check state laws governing nonprofit raffles. And remember to make it clear to participants that the IRS doesn't allow charitable deductions for raffle ticket purchases.

NO. 46

Naming Games

Sell naming rights to small school projects and reap big windfalls.

Funding Sources: Sponsorships

Potential Haul: > $5,000

Possible Partners/Sponsors: Corporate donors

SUCCESS SNAPSHOTS

⑤ Looking beyond big-dollar naming deals for sports stadiums and other facilities, which are out of reach to all but rich citizens and large local companies, many schools enable regular folks (and sometimes small businesses) to chip in and help name more modest projects. Selling small engraved plaques on the backs of auditorium seats is one of the most popular approaches. At California's Whittier High, for instance, donors could sponsor seats for $150, $250, $500, and $1,000, depending on their location in the theater, the *Tri-Valley Herald* reported ("School Fund-Raiser," 2004). Meanwhile, the public schools of Framingham, Massachusetts, sold plaques for middle school auditorium seats for $50 but bumped up the donation level to $100 and $250 in the high school, the *Boston Globe* reported (Heyman, 2006). And North Carolina's

Guilford Technical Community College sold $100 amphitheater seat sponsorships to enable average citizens to participate in an endowment fund drive that included much larger naming rights opportunities, the *News & Record* reported (Newsom, 2004). Said one donor, who included the phrase "Enjoy the show!" on her brass seat-back plaque, "It's so cool. It really gives you a good feeling. It's probably the only place my name will be forever."

⑤ Personalized decorative wall tiles and walkway bricks remain popular fundraising tools. Using a design created by an artisan parent, Anita Oaks School in Duarte, California, put up a wall of tiles that donors (or their children) could personalize by painting a picture in the middle, the *Pasadena Star-News* reported (Butko, 2003). Each tile went for $125. "They could buy it for a teacher, parent, or co-worker," an organizer suggested. "Or they could buy one in memory of alumni." The designer offered to paint tiles for any contributors who didn't want to do it themselves.

At Golden Sierra High in Garden Valley, California, an ambitious drive to upgrade sports facilities included selling sponsorships for tiles on an 8-foot-by-300-foot stadium wall, the *Sacramento Bee* reported (Gutierrez, 2005). The smallest tiles were available for $100, with prices rising from there. "In the absence of a guy with a big checkbook, we have a lot of small checkbooks," one organizer said.

North Carolina State University paid for library upgrades in part by selling personalized bricks for an outside walkway at $150–$250 each, the *Technician* reported (Windham, 2005). "Our donors are using it as a way to do something as a tribute or to recognize another family member," a fundraising official said. "One of the things we're trying to do is to have opportunities that are available to everyone." Added the library director, "A parent might buy one for a student's graduation or a few students might purchase a brick together."

⑤ Roll the dice by inviting local businesses and other organizations to sponsor a Monopoly-style board game. That's what marketing students at Monona Grove High at Cottage Grove/Monona, Wisconsin, did recently, the *Capital Times* reported (Saemann, 2006). Board spaces, which included business logos and contact details, went for $200–$400, while game cards cost $100. One local firm even ponied up to sponsor the play money—and the police officers' union chipped in for the Go to Jail spot. An art student designed the box cover, and the marketing team worked closely with business owners to make sure they were satisfied with the look of their spaces. About 300 of the resulting Cottage Grove-opoly games were then sold at the school and local retail outlets for $20 each. All told, the initiative netted more than $4,000. The school purchased the games from Michigan-based Pride Distributors, Inc., which specializes in supplying Your Town-opoly fundraisers. For more information, visit www.townopoly.net.

ADDED ATTRACTIONS

- Other possibilities for selling name plaques include water fountains; trophy cases; courtyard benches; bus seats; library chairs, carrels, and shelves; and even the cases for school-owned band instruments. Or what about creating a virtual Wall of Fame on your school's Web site?
- See Chapter 2, "Don't Try This at School," for tips on avoiding naming rights mishaps.

NO. 47
Give 'em the Boot

Enlist crossing guards and other members of the school community to ask passing motorists to drop donations into an outstretched boot.

Funding Sources: Donations

Potential Haul: < $1,000

Possible Partners/Sponsors: Corporate donors

SUCCESS SNAPSHOT

- Ⓢ A crossing guard at St. Joseph's School in Webster, Massachusetts, publicized one of the Catholic school's annual fundraisers by dressing as a cowboy every Friday for a month and asking motorists and pedestrians to drop pennies into a cowboy boot, the *Telegram & Gazette* reported (Hill, 2005). At the fundraising dinner—which extended the cowboy theme by dishing up barbecue grub—attendees were invited to guess the number of pennies in the boot. The person who came closest to the correct number won a door prize.

ADDED ATTRACTIONS

- Ⓢ Other possibilities include collecting cash in vintage moon boots to promote a *Napoleon Dynamite*–themed fundraiser, army boots for a military academy or school near a military base, hiking boots for an outdoorsy event, or even costumed superhero boots to kick off a super money-raising effort.
- Ⓢ Ask the police department to park a squad car in clear view a few blocks from school during this fundraiser so that motorists are on their best behavior when they arrive at the crosswalk.

NO. 48

Fee Parking

Allow teens to personalize school parking spaces for an annual surcharge.

Funding Sources: Auction proceeds

Potential Haul: > $5,000

Possible Partners/Sponsors: Art supply stores

SUCCESS SNAPSHOT

⑤ Several Texas high schools give students the opportunity to customize their parking spaces with artistic abandon in exchange for an annual fee, the *Fort Worth Star-Telegram* reported (Brown, 2006). Some students do little more than stencil their names on the spots; others paint full-blown murals or several smaller works centered on a theme. One senior recently decked out her space with pictures of Garfield the cartoon cat and his pals Odie and Pooky, while another paid homage to the Beatles. School mascots remain popular choices, and some students even bring in professional artists to burnish their spaces. The perk costs each teen $20 to $50 annually on top of standard parking fees. Some schools rake in nearly $20,000 a year with these fundraisers. Painting the spaces "gives kids some individuality, which is something teens have a keen interest in," one district spokesperson noted. Ground rules sometimes include using only school colors—and paint that can be washed away easily when classes end. Administrators also ban offensive language, symbols, and pictures. Most schools encourage teachers to decorate their spots as well—at no extra charge, of course.

NO. 49

Your Money or Your Time

Offer community members multiple ways to give.

Funding Sources: Pledges

Potential Haul: > $5,000

Possible Partners/Sponsors: Civic groups

SUCCESS SNAPSHOT

⑤ Why not hold a pledge drive that asks people to donate either money or time—or, if possible, both? Advertise your volunteer needs alongside requests to help fund important projects. Some folks don't have cash to spare for charitable causes, no matter how worthy. But they may gladly give the gift of their time if you make them feel welcome and valued. Not only is this a community-inclusive event, it will also remind residents at all income levels that the school will value their skills whenever they can pitch in.

NO. 50

Stunts Doubling

Cap off a successful fundraising effort by performing a silly stunt.

Funding Sources: Pledges

Potential Haul: > $5,000

Possible Partners/Sponsors: Corporate donors, civic groups

SUCCESS SNAPSHOTS

⑨ I'll end this round-up of creative fundraising ideas by attempting to raise some funds for a (somewhat) worthy cause: myself. Spur students to success by promising to perform one of the silly stunts outlined in my recent Corwin Press book *101 Stunts for Principals to Inspire Student Achievement* if they meet their fundraising goals. Favorite administrator stunts include shaving one's head (or facial hair); eating worms; kissing pigs; spending a morning on the school roof; trading places with a student for a day; taking a dip in a dunk tank; and dressing up as a gorilla, superhero, or popular storybook character. Heck, you don't even have to buy the book to see how well that last type of stunt motivates children. Just read the next item . . .

❸ Students at Kensington Elementary in Waxhaw, North Carolina, recently brought in nearly $5,500 for new books by reading for a cumulative total of 122,909 minutes as part of a two-week Read-a-Thon and Book Raiser, the *Charlotte Observer* reported (Hastings, 2006). Principal Rachel Clarke rewarded the kids by dressing up as Thing Two from Dr. Seuss's *The Cat in the Hat* and riding through the halls on a scooter. "It has been wonderful to see the excitement the children have for reading," she said. "They far surpassed our goal" of reading for 25,000 minutes during the challenge period.

ADDED ATTRACTIONS

❸ Sometimes the stunt itself drives the fundraising activity. That was the case at Community High in West Chicago, Illinois, where more than 2,100 students chipped in to a Turkey Contest, the *Chicago Daily Herald* reported (Hitzeman & Komperda, 2004). The teens dropped change and bills into cans representing different teachers. At the end of the fundraising period, the two faculty members with the most money in their cans were dubbed the winners. Their prize: roaming the halls in turkey costumes the day before Thanksgiving break. Five runners-up donned silly hats on the appointed day. The competition raised more than $1,600 for the Make-A-Wish Foundation.

❸ Fools on the Roof was the apt name for a fundraiser that stuck participants atop the Zanesville, Ohio, Wal-Mart until they each racked up at least $500 in pledges, the *Zanesville Times-Recorder* reported (Shipley, 2006). A fire department ladder truck stood by to help them down, and a local restaurant kept them well-fueled for several rounds of phone calls to potential donors. The event raises more than $10,000 annually for the American Cancer Society.

References

Abe, D. (2006, August 27). Bands ready to rock Stadium party. *News Tribune*, p. B1.

Alexander, K. (2004, March 29). Schools find help on eBay. *Los Angeles Times*, p. B5.

Anderson, B. (2003, October 22). Creative collectors: Parents finding innovative ways to replace traditional school fund-raisers. *The Oklahoman*, p. A17.

Anderson, N. (2006, February 19). Schools chief offers a record of unifying: Fundraising fight in Calif. shows philosophy of incoming Pr. George's leader. *Washington Post*, p. C1.

Austin, M. (2006, May 6). Car show benefits Head Start children. *Coshocton Tribune*, p. A5.

Avila, E. (2006, February 10). Pampering princesses: Girls Night Out in Tulare a great success as fundraiser for youth center. *Fresno Bee*, p. SVB2.

Ayala, E. M. (2004, October 30). Fund-raiser frightfully successful. *Fort Worth Star Telegram*, p. B1.

Ayala, J. (2006, June 3). Signs of change: Banners to replace junk food as student fundraisers. *Press-Enterprise*, p. B1.

Bach, L. K. (2003, October 12). Controversy stirs talk of school name change. *Las Vegas Review-Journal*, p. B1.

Ball, L. (2005, September 17). Bryan students gathering phones as fundraiser. *Spokesman-Review*, p. I3.

Barksdale, T. (2003, September 25). Youngster using scrapbooking fundraiser to help brain-tumor patients. *Winston-Salem Journal*, p. CJ1.

Bennett, A. (2006, February 15). "Red Wine & Blues." *San Bernardino County Sun*, p. B4.

Bennett, M. (2006, August 10). Kings of the Court tournament seeks best in basketball. *Palladium-Item*, p. B1.

Berkhahn, J. (2006, February 12). Golfers hit the links er, ice. *Wausau Daily Herald*, p. A3.

Bertagnoli, L. (2006, February 6). Auction bidders go for intangibles; Movie roles, celeb lunches enrich charities; buying an experience. *Crain's Chicago Business*, p. 39.

Berthiaume, E. (2006, May 25). Stroke of genius: Painting project to aid displaced artists. *Post-Crescent*, p. B1.

Bigelow, C. (2006, February 19). Bark & Whine a fetching good time. *San Francisco Chronicle*, p. D5.

Braly, A. P. (2006, March 14). Recycling of electronics aids nature center. *Chattanooga Times Free Press*, p. B1.

Brown, J. (2006, September 22). Art marks the spot: Customized parking spaces give students prime property. *Fort Worth Star-Telegram*, p. A1.

Burns, D. (2006a, September 1). Manning superintendent's calendar pose stirs storm: One parent says Schmiedeskamp's appearance amounts to soft-core porn, others defend action as charity minded. *Carroll Daily Times Herald*, p. 1.

Burns, D. (2006b, October 12). Manning Rotary Club turns international story into fund-raiser success. *Carroll Daily Times Herald*, p. 1.

Butko, T. (2003, April 6). School uses creative fund-raiser: Anita Oaks selling decorated tiles. *Pasadena Star-News*, p. B1.

Cardwell, J. (2006a, February 1). Students lend hand for day: For good cause, 8th-graders raffle selves off as aides. *Akron Beacon Journal*, p. B1.

Cardwell, J. (2006b, May 3). Creative folks host fundraisers. *Akron Beacon Journal*, p. B1.

Challender, M. (2006, June 10). Roll up the garage doors: New Jefferson tour offers peek inside snazzy spots. *Des Moines Register*, p. E3.

Chou, E. (2005, April 18). Slinging hamburgers for education. *San Gabriel Valley Tribune*, p. B1.

Clough, B. (2006, February 17). Bankrupt company delays payments: Scrip Advantage tells clients it expects to file for Chapter 11 next month. *Fresno Bee*, p. C1.

Conan, N. (Host). (2006, September 21). Schools seek new ways to raise funds. *Talk of the Nation*. National Public Radio. Available at www .npr.org/templates/story/story.php?storyId=6117456.

Cooke, C. (2006, January 13). Ringgold students set "Groucho" glasses record. *Chattanooga Times Free Press*, p. B1.

Cook-Romero, E. (2006, February 24). Finger foods for finger paints. *Santa Fe New Mexican*, p. PA40.

Cox, R. (2003, October 15). "Seneschal" serves the UAA team a Bizbee win: Annual event raises funds for adult literacy program. *Anchorage Daily News*, p. B5.

Crane, J. (2005, May 26). Vanity bear: Community art project will feature 40 life-size Kodiaks. *Spokesman-Review*, p. D1.

Daday, E. O. (2006, March 8). Fundraiser planners uncork wine tastings. *Chicago Daily Herald*, p. N4.

Danley-Greiner, K. (2006, July 4). Set the clock for Summerfest parade. *Des Moines Register*, p. R1.

Darvish, A. R. (2005, July 21). Smelly victory: Benefit bingo relies on barnyard byproducts. *Daily News of Los Angeles*, p. SC1.

De Jesus, J. (2005, November 17). Holiday homes open doors: Tour, tea and boutique is a fund-raiser for Moraga schools, library and parks. *Contra Costa Times*, p. F4.

Delaney, B. (2006, May 31). School camp out sparks a love of reading. *Asbury Park Press*, p. F4.

Dicken, G. (2006, August 25). Volleyball team members wait tables. *Chronicle-Tribune*, p. A5.

Ebert, R. (2006, April 28). Virtues of *Akeelah* go beyond spelling. *Chicago Sun-Times*, p. 28.

Erickson, T. (2006, April 12). Stewart booked? Oops. *Deseret Morning News*, p. B1.

Esparza, S. (2005, March 16). Scrapbookers cut, paste to help schools: Livonia district wants to make the fund-raiser that generated $3,000 an annual event. *Detroit News*, p. J12.

Estrada, S. M. (2006, March 1). College circus goes to school. *St. Petersburg Times*, p. NT1.

Ferris, J. (2006, January 17). Net result: World record; UNC, Duke students shoot hoops for kids. *Herald-Sun*, p. A1.

Fox, L. (2005, September 9). This is no ordinary school fundraiser: Carroll ISD auction items include 103-inch TV, lease on a Lexus. *Dallas Morning News*, p. B11.

Frasieur, D. (2006, June 20). Windows and wine set the stage for fundraiser: Buchanan Art Center seeks help to pay off loan. *South Bend Tribune*, p. E1.

Gallagher, L. (2006, May 25). The littlest golfers: Wilson kindergartners hold golf-themed fundraiser. *South Bend Tribune*, p. E2.

Garton, N. (2006, February 24). School fundraiser taps experts from sharks, songs, football. *Tennessean*, p. D1.

Gaunt, J. (2004, September 23). School's fund-raiser's so good you could eat it up. *Chicago Daily Herald*, p. N3.

Gibson, E. (2006, September 29). Florida students read aloud together for record books. *Miami Herald*, p. A2.

Graham, D. (2005, July 3). Race doesn't yield a duck worth $1M, but shelter does raise more than $50,000. *Post and Courier*, p. B3.

Greene, T. (2006, July 22). Here are a few animal-related events coming up in the area. *Montgomery Advertiser*, p. D1.

Groves, M. (2004, January 22). Parents divided over proposal to pool fundraising: Santa Monica-Malibu district official wants affluent campuses to share contributions. *Los Angeles Times*, p. B4.

Guinness world records 2007. (2006). London: Guinness Media.

Gutierrez, M. (2005, November 2). Still in the money, without big donors: From selling naming rights to creating a nonprofit group, these schools find a way. *Sacramento Bee*, p. C1.

Hanna, R. (2004, March 4). "They just go out and do it" at Schilling Farms Middle. *Commercial Appeal*, p. CL11.

Harris, C. (2006, February 24). Hole-in-one insurance policies provide safety net for glitzy tournament contests. *Memphis Business Journal*, p. 12.

Hastings, L. (2006, April 2). Students hit the books for Kensington read-a-thon: Kids logged 122,909 minutes in 2-week schoolwide challenge. *Charlotte Observer*, p. U6.

Hernan, P. (2000, April 20). Gun worries unabated: Clarion student with chocolate gun to be charged. *Pittsburgh Post-Gazette*, p. A1.

Hernando PTO gives moms a night out. (2006, April 28). *Commercial Appeal*, p. DSB6.

Hewson, P. (2006, April 3). Brown's Bruno wins title, dismantles Quaker. *Brown Daily Herald*, p. 1.

Heyman, S. (2006, June 15). Fund-raiser for arts in schools. *Boston Globe*, p. GW2.

Hill, J. L. (2005, January 17). This boot's made for collecting: Crossing guard "cowboy" boosts Webster school fund-raiser. *Telegram & Gazette*, p. B6.

Hitzeman, H., & Komperda, J. (2004, November 17). School fund-raiser to have teachers talking turkey. *Chicago Daily Herald*, p. N1.

Hoffman, G. (2006, February 28). School fundraiser will feature fathers. *Pasadena Star-News*, p. B1.

Howard, A. (2005, October 25). Artists design chairs for school fund-raiser. *Cincinnati Enquirer*, p. B3.

Hudspeth, J. (2006, September 20). Sail back in time at Liberty Hall. *Lexington Herald Leader*, p. C2.

Hughes, K. (2004, September 2). Nonprofits turn to fund-raising twists: From karaoke to cow chips, it's all about keeping support base. *Dallas Morning News*, p. S1.

Hussain, R. (2006, April 13). Not this Jon Stewart, that Jon Stewart. *Chicago Sun-Times*, p. 5.

In the doghouse: Annual home tour includes designer "canine casitas" for sale. (2006, February 18). *Desert Sun*, p. F1.

Ismail, R. (2004, March 24). Kids' chores scoring cash for library: S. Brunswick building to grow. *Home News Tribune*, p. R1.

Jackson, D. (2006, March 30). Soothing for the soul: Tea parties bring back a well-mannered era. *Detroit Free Press*, p. CFP12.

Jardina, E. (2006, April 22). Garden parties: Out of the rain, into the backyards, it's time to tour homes. *Inside Bay Area*, p. 16.

Jennings, C. (2006, November 3). McTeacher's Night at McDonald's. *Daily Home*, p. B2.

Jeweler to raise money for crime commission. (1999, May 2). *Tulsa World*, p. H1.

Joachim, J. (2003). *Beyond the bake sale: The ultimate school fund-raising book*. New York: St. Martin's Press.

Kahn, C. (Reporter). (2004, July 6). Public schools' bids for private money raise questions. *All Things Considered*. National Public Radio. Archived at www.npr.org/templates/story/story.php?storyId=3173016.

Kan, M. (2006, May 6). Playing for the troops: Teachers compete with eighth-graders. *Kansas City Star*, p. A12.

Kane, L. (2006, February 9). Spellathon raises money, students' spirits: A total of 7,274 words were spelled correctly, earning the school $2,500 in pledges. *Des Moines Register*, p. B1.

Kay, L. F. (2005, November 15). Odds are against school fundraisers: Raffles, bingo, similar activities break some Md. systems' rules against games of chance. *Baltimore Sun*, p. A1.

Kays, H. (2006, July 17). Circus raises money for class. *Herald News*, p. B1.

Keenan, P. (2006, February 9). Farmington opens house and books for families. *Commercial Appeal*, p. GM4.

Kimball, J. (2004, March 11). Web site lets donors specify school gifts. *Star Tribune*, p. B7.

Kolben, D. (2006, May 15). Where to get a date with an Olsen twin. *New York Sun*, p. 1.

Kormanik, B. (2005, December 12). School fund-raisers become more creative than baking a cake: Some produce a product to sell while others purge the hassle of selling. *Florida Times-Union*, p. A1.

Krieger, L. M. (2006, February 5). Books, books, books! Children's writers, artists help the next generation. *San Jose Mercury News*, p. B1.

Kumar, K. (2002, April 19). One for the records: Sixth-graders have assembled what may be the world's largest pop-up book. *Star Tribune*, p. B1.

Lawrence, J. (2004, November 21). Raising their efforts: School fund-raisers aren't just about candy anymore. There are more options and the money is often a saving grace. *Orange County Register*, p. I1.

Lei, S. (2006, October 16). "Blisterama!" raises $2,500. *Bellingham Herald*, p. A12.

Lilyestrom, B. (2005, October 19). Trash becomes cash in school fundraiser. *Telegram & Gazette*, p. B3.

Lopez, R. (2005, July 4). Lawn ornaments? No, fund-raisers. *Times Union*, p. B1.

Lou, L. (2005, December 6). Teens on toes for a cause: Students will present 16 routines from ballet to hip-hop for hospital cancer work. *Press Enterprise*, p. B3.

Lovato, T. E. (2006, July 9). Musical chairs: Teens get together for event to benefit Susan's Legacy. *Albuquerque Journal*, p. E5.

Lucadamo, K. (2005, June 7). Parents go dough nuts: School fund-raisers rake in spare change to 500G. *New York Daily News*, p. 30.

Lykins, L. (2006, July 12). Enjoy a $10 spa treat, help a kid. *St. Petersburg Times*, p. N11.

Malibu Family Wines hosts sixth annual Harvest & Crush event honoring City Hearts: Kids say "yes" to the arts. (2006, September 14). Market Wire. Available at www.marketwire.com/mw/release_html_b1?release_id=163039.

Maller, P. (2004a, November 12). Sharp seller: School fund-raiser with knife halted; Weapons ban keeps students from peddling donated fishing kits. *Milwaukee Journal Sentinel*, p. B1.

Maller, P. (2004b, November 13). School sets rules for selling kits: Adults, not Germantown students, will handle fund-raiser item with knife. *Milwaukee Journal Sentinel*, p. B1.

Maraghy, M. (2006, May 6). Art Guild decorates stands for school band fundraiser: They'll be auctioned off at Orange Park Junior High's spring band concert. *Florida Times-Union*, p. M18.

Marsh, H. (2006, July 27). Get your pooch ready for Pet Walk, Bark in the Park. *Palladium-Item*, p. B4.

Matzelle, C. (2004, February 28). Creative fund-raisers have a serious purpose: Students, teachers put minds, fingers to work collecting money for their schools. *Plain Dealer*, p. B1.

McDaniel, C. (2004, November 12). Chamber fund-raiser will relive prom night: Adults with tuxes and gowns will turn back the clock tonight at Indiana Downs. *Indianapolis Star*, p. S1.

McNeish, J. (2006, February 12). Wine event to benefit Post Falls schools. *Spokesman-Review*, p. D6.

Medina, J. (2005, October 21). Taking playhouses to next level: An auction of miniature homes benefits HomeAid Orange County, which helps transitionally homeless. *Orange County Register*, p. LP1.

Meehan, M. (2006, September 26). PoochFest grew from one pet owner's love of animals. *St. Louis Post-Dispatch*, p. B1.

Mehta, S. (2006, September 27). Sorry, cupcake, you're no longer welcome in class: To fight student obesity, educators opt for celebratory carrots and books. *Los Angeles Times*, p. A1.

Miltner, K. (2005, December 20). Straight talk on wine. *Rochester Democrat and Chronicle*, p. C1.

Moore, J. C. (2005, September 17). Parents take school fundraisers upscale: Business savvy raises events to whole new level. *Ventura County Star*, p. A1.

Morrison, K. G. (2006, July 31). Fashionably challenged: Armed with $100 budgets, designers battle to win contest. *Detroit News*, p. E1.

Murphy, D. (2004, October 15). Fund-racing for schools: Parents' games give San Carlos students a leg up. *San Francisco Chronicle*, p. F1.

Murray, K. W. (2006, September 25). A king of entertainment. *Poughkeepsie Journal*, p. D1.

Nacelewicz, T. (2004, June 7). Group of school boosters creates hi-tech alternative to bake sale: People who sell items through a classified-ad Web site give part of the profit to Falmouth schools. *Portland Press Herald*, p. B1.

Nagata, K. (2006, June 7). Starry, Starry Night a success. *Sarasota Herald-Tribune*, p. BV4.

Nakashima, R. (2006, August 31). Las Vegas area school foundation accepts strip club donation. The Associated Press. Available from the *Las Vegas Sun* at www.lasvegassun.com/sunbin/stories/nevada/2006/aug/30/083010420.html.

Newsom, J. (2004, September 12). For $ale: Naming college property no longer only for rich. *News & Record*, p. A1.

Nichols, S. (2006, October 6). Dogs invited to Bark in Park. *Greenville News*, p. A1.

Nicholson, L. (2000, February 17). Chip-ping in for schools: A cow chip bingo event gives schools a few good plops' worth of assistance. *Orange County Register*, p. BP3.

Nighttime-naturalist program to investigate stars. (2006, March 24). *Orlando Sentinel*, p. G9.

Noguchi, S. (2006, September 5). A beach house will go to lucky winner. *San Jose Mercury News*, p. B1.

Obmascik, M. (1997, September 16). If chips are down, it's bingo. *Denver Post*, p. B1.

Ogden, K. (2004, November 16). Shhhh! The mosquitoes are sleeping. *Great Falls Tribune*, p. M12.

Oliver, A. (2005, February 6). "Cow bingo" scores. *Commercial Appeal*, p. DS1.

O'Toole, A. (2005, November 3). Fundraiser puts gingerbread at center stage. *Wichita Eagle*, p. E1.

O'Toole, C. (2006, May 3). Chairs for charity: A creative fundraiser for Fulton YMCA. *Post-Standard*, p. B1.

Oyola, M. (2006, October 26). Fundraisers go to extremes to attract big bucks. *St. Louis Post-Dispatch*, p. E1.

Paras, A. (2006, March 2). Circus at school: Colleton kids enjoy Big Top fundraiser. *Post and Courier*, p. E1.

Peattie, P. (2006, May 20). For this fundraiser, men worked while women happily took in the sights. *San Diego Union-Tribune*, p. E10.

Pedicini, S. (1993, October 31). Designer homes will open doors for tour. *Orlando Sentinel*, p. K5.

Peoples, S. (2006, February 15). Strike a pose: Model behavior at school fundraiser. *Providence Journal*, p. C1.

Pieper, L. (2006, January 26). Library's collection grows with students: Terrace Elementary's birthday book program puts kids' names inside donated selections. *Des Moines Register,* p. B1.

Pina, A. A. (2001, October 16). On the mooo-ve: For Martin, a delay of game. *Providence Journal-Bulletin,* p. C1.

Poltilove, J. (2006, February 11). Relocated book fair a fun fundraiser for Mabry. *Tampa Tribune,* p. ST4.

Pope, E. (2005, March 11). "Top Gun" ride lures bidders to auction: Entertainment or fantasy experiences generate high interest at school fund-raiser. *Detroit News,* p. C2.

Powers, N. C. (2006, March 16). Class on the course: Farmington Hills students learn math and science by designing mini-golf. *Detroit Free Press,* p. CFP8.

Prom fund-raiser set for Hatton woman. (2006, March 29). *Grand Forks Herald,* p. B1.

PTA fund-raiser brings circus to town. (2003, September 4). *Lincolnwood Review,* p. 5.

Randle, M. (2005, October 21). Grab your camera, map for a hunt around town. *Chicago Daily Herald,* p. N1.

Ranganathan, D. (2006, January 1). Gallery show hopes to teach students the art of the deal: Turning high school painters, sculptors into professionals is what 5th annual event is about. *Sacramento Bee,* B1.

Reveron, M. (2004, September 30). McDonald's hosts McTeacher's Night™ school fundraisers throughout region. PR Newswire.

Rhoades, B. (1999, March 18). Contest spells education for kids, cash for school. *Newport Beach Light,* p. 2.

Richwine, E. (2004, January 10). Participants ready to bear cold for icy fund-raiser. *Journal and Courier,* p. B12.

Rivera, C. (2006, May 21). Bake sales go strictly black tie: Elite academies have elevated fundraising to high art in order to tap well-heeled parents. *Los Angeles Times,* p. A1.

Rock, C. (2005, March 24). More than a thousand kids accept junior high's fitness challenge: Event raises funds for P.E. department. *Daily News of Los Angeles,* p. SC1.

Rodgers, A. (2005, September 11). They're going to a pajama party! *Palm Beach Post,* p. D5.

Rollin' in the dough: Rolling Stones-signed guitars go for $20,000 each at Stanley Clark School fundraiser. (2006, March 8). *South Bend Tribune,* p. E3.

Rosen, D. (2003, September 11). Foundation cooks up creative fund-raisers for Lamar teachers. *Houston Chronicle,* p. TW1.

Rubin, N. (2006, July 14). Let's get the vote out for Sparty to beat the tail off that furry badger from Wis. *Detroit News,* p. E1.

Ryan, A. (2006, April 6). Demand for tickets to Portland's Street of Eames modern home tour tops supply. *Daily Journal of Commerce*, p. 20.

Ryan, A., & Kaye K. (2005, March 16). Teen charged with selling marijuana brownies: Police say student sold goodies outside school cafeteria. *Sun-Sentinel*, p. B1.

Ryman, A. (2003, November 18). Arcadia bars "servant/slave" fundraiser: Students fume. *Arizona Republic*, p. B1.

Saemann, K. (2006, February 17). Monopoly-like game makes grade: Marketing students bring Cottage Grove's businesses on board. *Capital Times*, C1.

Sayer, D. (2006, August). Youth circus to give Kennebunkport shows: Circus Smirkus will perform four times to benefit Kennebunkport's Consolidated School. *Portland Press Herald*, p. B4.

Scalf, A. (2003, December 21). School's Charity Week gets wacky. *Chicago Daily Herald*, p. N1.

Scholten, J. (2006, May 7). Paws for fashion: Kids' animal T-shirts to help homeless pets. *Atlanta Journal-Constitution*, p. ZH9.

School fund-raiser asks sponsors to take a seat. (2004, November 1). *Whittier Daily News*, p. B2.

Sederstrom, J. (2005, July 6). Student fundraiser fills yards with pink. *Kansas City Star*, p. T1.

Shadia, M. (2006, October 13). Unique fundraiser mixes yoga, belly dancing, fashion. *Inland Valley Daily Bulletin*, p. 1.

Shakes, F., & De Los Reyes, J. D. (2006, January 29). Golf for fun and funds. *Sun-Sentinel*, p. B3.

Sherry, C. (2003, October 20). Marion's "Transyl-Maze-ia" scares up some needed cash. *Post-Crescent*, p. E1.

Shipley, T. (2006, April 1). It's for a good cause, no foolin'. *Zanesville Times-Recorder*, p. A1.

Shores, K. D. (2006, February 3). Kids eschew candy sales to raise cash for field trips. *Sun-Sentinel*, p. C8.

Shrieves, L. (2003, January 16). Mascots go to bat: Unheralded, unknown, unusual—for one day they step off sidelines onto center stage. *Orlando Sentinel*, p. E1.

Shriner, T. (2006, November 9). All dolled up: Fashion show offers All-American fun; Dolls dress up with a historical flair. *Times-Picayune*, p. 99.

Silkin, S. (1999, September 21). Rotarians create larger labyrinth, add scary hayride; Last year's benefit raised $20,000 for Boys & Girls Club; puzzle will be a third larger this year. *Ventura County Star*, p. B1.

Siskin, D. (2000, November 17). Charities spice up fund-raisers: To get the most out of giving, nonprofits take new options. *Chattanooga Times Free Press*, p. E1.

Sodders, L. M. (2005, December 4). Homes for the holidays: Charity fundraiser shows off residents' Yuletide décor. *Daily News of Los Angeles*, p. N4.

Sowers, C. (2005, May 21). Giant guitars are starting to take shape for auction. *Arizona Republic*, p. B4.

Spivak, A. (2005, December 18). Gingerbread houses worth every bite. *Kansas City Star*, p. F6.

Student facing drug charges. (2002, December 7). *Columbus Dispatch*, p. B4.

Szpaller, K. (2005, March 31). Left of the dial. *Missoula Independent*, p. 6.

Tea Party benefit scheduled today. (2006, October 7). *State Journal-Register*, p. L14.

Teen admits to lacing cake with hash. (2004, February 16). United Press International.   Available at www.highbeam.com/doc/1P1 -91169813.html.

Ter Maat, S. (2006, September 16). Big top success: Circus fundraiser earns $10,000 for Dist. 59 Education Foundation. *Chicago Daily Herald*, p. N1.

Thompson, A. (2005, May 12). "Romeo and Juliet" to take the stage. *Times-Picayune*, p. RS1.

Thompson, A. M. (2004, September 9). Cypress School PTO tightens rules. *Tulare Advance-Register*, p. A1.

Thorpe, C. (2006, April 19). Recycles day aims to raise awareness. *Sun-Sentinel*, p. CN5.

Tuohy, J. (2006, October 25). Spooks relish haunting maze visitors: Haunted corn maze at Danville orchard raises money to help others. *Indianapolis Star*, p. B2.

Vaishnav, A. (2004, September 5). Going beyond bake sales: From hiring comedians and holding silent auctions, parents get creative—and raise thousands of dollars for schools. *Boston Globe*, p. B8.

Wai, L. (2002, May 17). Chipping in for good goal: Women's over-50 soccer team offers unique fund-raiser. *Honolulu Advertiser*, p. C7.

Wallace, N. (2005, June 9). A surge in online giving. *Chronicle of Philanthropy*, p. 7.

Wasserman, M. (2006a, February 16). Families show love in words, pictures: Parents and students will create memories at Brooksville Elementary's Scrapbook Night. *St. Petersburg Times*, p. B1.

Wasserman, M. (2006b, February 16). Reading has its reward: There will be free yearbooks for all at Chocachatti Elementary School, all because of a fair. *St. Petersburg Times*, p. B2.

Westphal, M. (2006a, October 16). Heritage to the brim. *Rockford Register Star*, p. G6.

Westphal, M. (2006b, October 30). It's a girl's world. *Rockford Register Star,* p. G5.

Whitmire, L. (2006, February 12). Girls and their dolls do some primping at tea party. *Mansfield News Journal,* p. C3.

Wiener, J. (2006, March 25). Teens craft a fashion show for their homeless peers. *Sacramento Bee,* p. B1.

Wilcox, S. (2006, February 15). "Men Who Cook" dish up delectable event. *Bradenton Herald,* p. 8.

Williams, C. (2006, October 25). Event serves up DARE funds: Fowlerville schools hope to collect $1,000 to keep anti-drug program running. *Detroit News,* p. B4.

Wilmot, P. (2005, May 8). A buffalo is born. *Great Falls Tribune,* p. BH23.

Wilson, J. D. (2006, July 20). Street ball tournament aims to benefit children. *Myrtle Beach Sun-News,* p. C1.

Wilson, L. (2004, October 18). Students can raise funds their own ways. *Chicago Daily Herald,* p. N1.

Windham, C. (2005, January 25). N.C. State library patrons get opportunity to leave mark. *Technician,* p. 1.

Wine-tasting raises $7,000 for schools. (2006, February 9). *Asbury Park Press,* p. M5.

Winters, W. (2005, February 8). Artists create storybook chairs for Key School fund-raiser. *The Capital,* p. C1.

Womack, P. (2004, December 19). Riverdale auction raises $12,000: School's fund-raiser brings support for reader program. *Commercial Appeal,* p. GM12.

Wrestlers available for household chores during Rent-a-Wrestler Day Saturday. (2006, May 18). *Topics,* p. A3.

Zezima, K. (2006, June 28). Goo and Fluff prevail in battle over lunches. *New York Times,* p. A18.

Zuckerman, F. B. (2006, April 16). Egads! E-waste! What's to be done with the mountains of our discarded electronics? *Providence Journal,* p. J1.